FATHERS
AND
CHILDREN

FATHERS AND CHILDREN

Life Lessons On Loving And Living

by Kyron Jackson

Fathers and Children
by Kyron Jackson

Published by Fathers and Children Book
www.FATHERSandChildrenBOOK.com

THE HOLY BIBLE, NEW INTERNATIONAL VERSION®, NIV® Copyright © 1973, 1978,
1984, 2011 by Biblica, Inc.® Used by permission. All rights reserved worldwide.

Scripture quotations marked (NLT) are taken from the Holy Bible, New Living Translation,
copyright © 1996, 2004, 2007 by Tyndale House Foundation. Used by permission
of Tyndale House Publishers, Inc., Carol Stream, Illinois 60188. All rights reserved.

The ESV® Bible (The Holy Bible, English Standard Version®) copyright © 2001
by Crossway, a publishing ministry of Good News Publishers. ESV® Text Edition: 2011.
The ESV® text has been reproduced in cooperation with and by permission
of Good News Publishers. Unauthorized reproduction of this publication is prohibited.
All rights reserved.

Scripture taken from the New King James Version®.
Copyright © 1982 by Thomas Nelson. Used by permission. All rights reserved.

© 2015 Kyron Jackson
All rights reserved. No portion of this book may be reproduced in any form without
permission from the publisher, except as permitted by U.S. copyright law.
For permissions contact: support@FATHERSandChildrenBOOK.com

Printed in the United States of America
First Printing, 2015

Paperback Book ISBN: 978-0-9969015-0-5

Fathers and Children Book Publishing

*For my wife Portia and children Johannah and Jessica,
thank you for allowing God to love me through you*

*For Birth fathers, Biological fathers, Adoptive fathers,
Father-in-laws, Foster fathers, Social fathers,
Father-figures, Step father's, Dada's,
Daddy's, Papa/Pappa's , Papasita's, Pa's,
Pap's, Pop's, and Baby daddy's —
the world is a better place because of you*

Acknowledgements

I would like to show my gratitude to the spiritual editor of this book, Pastor Lucious Hicks IV. You are endowed with precious gifts of wisdom, perspective, knowledge, and prayer and are uniquely positioned for maximum impact in the body of Christ. You're an exemplary father and a leader among men. Thank you for being a friend.

To Daphne Parsekian, my deep gratitude for your expertise and time in polishing up my manuscript.

I wish to present my special thanks to Kiryl for your gifts in making this book look great through graphic design, layout, and its overall look and feel.

To Donovan Kilgore, thank you for your photography and video talent—keep moving forward.

I would like to pay my regards to Meg Meeker for inspiring me to move forward in my calling; you never know where the seeds you plant will take root and produce fruit.

I would like to express my wholehearted gratitude to my family for your continued support, love, and prayers: Brenda Lee-Richardson & Poppa Jon, Albert & Jessical Jones, Urica & Patricia Jackson, Zyrun & Gretchen Jackson.

I would like to take a special moment to honor my father, Jessie B. Jackson (no, not the politician)

I would like to pay special thankfulness, warmth, and appreciation to the persons below who helped me become the father I am today:

- Leaders and mentors at Faithful Central Bible Church. Bishop Kenneth C. Ulmer, Pastor Steve Johnson, Bishop Sheridan McDaniel, Pastor Kasey Whitney, and Dr. Nicole LaBeach

- My peers and co-laborers in Christ: Twenty20 Young Adult Ministry (love you, leadership team!), Deeply Rooted Bible Study, Takeover Youth Ministry, Union Rescue Mission Ministry Team

- To Marriage Gang: Ameys, Whites, Shaws, Marshalls, Colliers, Dantus', Tylers, Howards, Jacksons, Hills, Weavers, Thompsons, Colliers

- To the Peters, Brown's, and my extended family—Go Jags!

- Distinguished Gentlemen of Alpha Phi Alpha Fraternity, Inc.: Epsilon Mu, Eta Sigma Lambda

- First Providence Missionary Baptist Church: Pastor Artis T. Lanier, Reginald Williams, Cool Cliff "Double CC" Roberts

- To "The Crew", Chris Hayes, my close friends, and my loved ones, who keep believing in me.

To my sweet daughters Johannah Grace and Jessica Joy Jackson, you two bring me instant joy. Without you this book wouldn't be possible. Dad will always love you.

Finally, a special thank you to my wife, Portia. Thank you for giving me the time, space, and encouragement to write this book. I love you and am a better man because of you. I wouldn't want to do life with anyone else. Cheers, to "the best us".

Table of Contents

Preface xv
Introduction 1
01. The Father Gives You Just Enough So You Remember Home 5
02. Trust the Father's Hands, They are Conditioned to Care for You 9
03. The Father's Gifts are Intended for Specific Seasons 13
04. Children are a Reflection of Their Father's Love 17
05. Obedience to the Father Comes with Liberty. 21
06. The Father Reminds Us It's Going to be Okay 25
07. The Father Knows What You Can Handle 29
08. The Father's Children Know His Voice. 33
09. When the Father Calls, Where are You? 37
10. You are in the Father's Plans, Faults and All 41
11. The Father Writes Down His Love for You. 45
12. Testing the Father's Limits 49
13. The Father Can Handle Your Anger. 53
14. The Father Comes to the Children's Level to Better Understand . . . 57
15. The Father's Thoughts are Above Our Thoughts 61
16. The Father Knows What It Takes to Get Your Attention 65
17. The Father Opens and Closes Doors 69
18. The Father Does What His Children Cannot Do 73
19. The Father's Gifts Come with Responsibility. 77
20. What are You Keeping From the Father? 81
21. There is No Hiding from The Father 85
22. The Father Has Us In Places to Influence Others 89
23. The Great and Terrible Father 93
24. In a World of Noise, The Father Knows His Children's Cries. 97
25. In The Father's Wisdom, He Gives His Children
Everything In Due Time. 101
26. Sometimes The Father Doesn't Make "It" Easy
So You Won't Take "It" For Granted 105

27. What The Father Has Prepared For You Is Only For You. 109
28. Father, Keep Your Hand On Me 113
29. The Father Protects Us From Hurting Ourselves. 117
30. Mature Children — Be Fed, Feed Yourself, Feed Others,
and Serve. 121
31. The Fathers Love Will Not Reinforce Your Mess 125
32. May The Lord Our Father, Turn His Face Towards You,
and Give You Peace. 129
33. The Father Provides Everything We Need 133
34. It Brings The Father Joy to Hear His Children Speak His Words. . . 137
35. Sometimes The Father Says Wait, Hold On, Stop. 141
36. The Father First Wants You to Handle The Last Thing
He Gave You 145
37. Our Worship Grabs The Father's Heart 149
38. The Father's War Cry 153
39. The Father Gives You What's Best For You 157
40. Childlike Complaining Can Cause You To Miss
The Father's Blessings 161
41. Consistently Checking In With The Father 165
42. As The Father Has Provided Before, He Will Provide
For You Again 169
43. The Father Knows Your Unique Cry. 173
44. I Want To Be Where The Father Is. 177
45. The Father Loves To See His Children Using
The Gifts He Gave Them 181
46. You Will Find Rest In The Father's Arms 185
47. The Father Helps You Do What You Can't Do Alone 189
48. Everything In The House Belongs to The Father,
He Can Do as He Pleases 193
49. The Fathers Children are In His Hands, On His Mind,
and In His Plans 197
50. The Father Loves to Hear The Voices Of His Children 201
51. The Father Uses Things to Draw Us Closer. 205
52. Thank You Father. 209
Conclusion 213
Certificate of Completion. 215
Pictures. 217
Index. 223

Welcome to
Fathers and Children

*"We have a Father, and He cares
about our internal world —
issues of motive, issues of fear,
issues of validation."*

— John Eldredge

FATHERS
AND
CHILDREN

Preface

When I was kid, like everyone else in the world, I was curiously searching for the purpose and meaning of my life. I wanted to know what impact I would have on the world, in what direction I should take my journey, and, of course, what I would be when I grew up.

What I quickly realized as the oldest boy in my family (I have an older sister and two younger brothers) is that my "rites of passage" process would include providing manly guidance to my younger brothers since our father was not in the home. My mom raised us to be respectable, God-fearing, and productive citizens, which is some kind of a miracle for a single parent of four children in the inner cities of Los Angeles.

I've always been a friendly guy (my name means "King of Friendship"), so it came naturally for me to see, by way of friendships, how there wasn't much fatherly guidance for many of my buddies either. I can clearly remember during my middle school and high school years how it was common among my friends not to have their fathers in the home. In fact, it was quite exceptional, even noteworthy, if I met someone who did! I can recall responding to one kid who I thought was exceptional with "Wow, both of your parents are still married? And your DAD is still there? What is it like to have them both together? Don't you feel weird?" Oh the irony of life.

From my childhood experience of being the responsible bigger brother, I became accustomed to also helping other young guys. Most of them were inner-city, predominantly black males who needed wisdom, resources, and positivity to help cope with the hardships of learning how to be a man without one being present. My experience of growing up in a fatherless home coupled with my passion for helping guys and an uncanny gift of wisdom led me to continue serving in similar roles throughout my life. Whether it be in church, at a park and recreation facility, or in college through my fraternity, Alpha Phi Alpha, I've always gravitated towards brotherhood, mentorship, and progress. It was during this time that I thought I found the answer to the purpose question of my life: I am to be an influence for young men like myself and to show them life beyond the inner city and options for a better life through God and higher education.

I continued to grow beyond college and went on with my professional life. In my college years, I had left the church for a while and had begun to feel disconnected with the core of who I am. Now in my early professional years, with the help of my friends, I returned to church and got involved again with the youth, among other ministries, believing this was where God intended me to be. Since then, I stayed involved with the youth for over 10 years in different capacities, and I just knew this was it—I'd found my lane in life!

While serving in the youth ministry I became more heavily involved in church and grew in my spiritual development. I started by becoming a minister, then a youth co-pastor, and ultimately the young adult pastor at Faithful Central Bible Church. I loved it. My years at the "Takeover" youth ministry were peppered with young men discipleship groups at my home, in gyms, in coffee houses, and at church. This continued throughout my time pastoring our collegiate and young professionals in our "Twenty20" young adult ministry.

Growing up shepherding these groups allowed me the privilege of watching young boys become young men, and it grew my understanding of what I understood my purpose to be. God was still calling me to reach the youth, specifically the young male (and in my mind at the time, the young black male), but the way I believe He was calling me to do so was through the young adult male as a role model. This way I could leverage the older "cool kids" influence and help facilitate the youth to feel understood and eventually become interested in the small group relationships where real change can be made.

So I went "all in" on this calling to equip young adult men to be role models by facilitating two to three small groups per year. Each group would have ten to twenty participants, maybe a couple co-facilitators, and would continue for eight to twelve weeks. I believed the more I could equip these young adult men, ages 18 to 29, to work hard, dream big, and live righteously by Christ, the more I could change or broaden their perspective on what God asks us to do with our lives as champions. I believed the more young adult men I could sharpen to influence the even younger generation, the better I could exponentially expand my reach toward the calling and purpose that God had planned for me. This was my life for a decade.

Today I believe God has revealed to me with better clarity the bigger picture purpose He's been developing within me. God has shown me that each time I've "found" His purpose for my life, I have only seen a dimly lit version of it, and one day the full panoramic view of it will emerge. The bigger picture, the deeper calling, and the clearer purpose He's now revealed to me is to not only to reach the youth, or the young adult man, or even "men in general" of any particular ethnicity but to reach the father. He's calling me to reach through the father, through the family construct, to the son, and from the son to reach the world.

This call on my life is designed to have a haloing effect on the community around us. By reaching the father as a means of building up the son, the love and respect for our daughters will naturally increase in the process. As fathers, we in turn will pick up the confidence of our wives and women when they see our effort and level of involvement. We'll pick up our neighborhoods because we care about the safety and direction of our next generation. We'll pick up the morality of our communities and cities along with our accountability of statesmen to better govern our society. By doing so, we'll inevitably pick up our nation and, ultimately, our world.

I once wrestled with the thought of why hadn't God called me to pour into and through the lives of individual men? It seemed to be more logical for me to move from children to young adults, from young adults to men, then from men to fathers. Then He showed me through the exercises and lessons in this book, *Fathers and Children*, that fathers have more "skin in the game" when it comes to the greater interests of society. A man can be very selfish and only concerned about his personal well being, his upward advancement, his influence, and his gain of power because he doesn't have dependents to be accountable for. He only has to look out for himself, so he primarily promotes his own interests and doesn't have a strong incentive to participate in the collective discipleship model. Obviously, this isn't true with all men, but in general, there is a societal expectation and construct of independence for men, a sort of "I can do it on my own" or "Rambo" persona that supports an "every man for themselves" ideology.

But the father comes from a different perspective and understanding of inter-relational dependencies. The father uses the lens of his children to see the inherent bond between himself and society. He knows the responsibility of modeling appropriate behavior, giving proper instruction, observing neighborly conduct, and correcting unacceptable patterns. Since parenting is so humbling, a father recognizes there are things in society he does not know, but he allows himself to grow while he guides and gains a new perspective along the way.

So there's a built-in, native model of discipleship in fatherhood. As responsible fathers, we want what's best for our children, and we realize our children are not going to grow up isolated from the world. For this reason, when our children are on the playground, at school, around the neighborhood, or with family members, we not only observe the behavior of our children but the behavior of the children around our children. We try our best to negotiate appropriate social behavior with other parents, spouses, significant others, friends, and people we casually meet. There's an inherent concern for our society. A concern for a better future. A concern for better children. A concern for better families. A concern for better fathers. A concern for better marriages. A concern for better communities. A concern for better states, better nations, and, ultimately, a better world. An all encompassing concern, just like Our Father's.

This book has fifty-two lessons, one for each week of the year, and is loosely written in chronological order. Lessons that don't have a specific time reference in them may have been written in a different sequence but the heart of them fits better in this order.

I pray this book connects with you by reaching through your mind, grabbing your heart, and giving it a reason to turn towards your children in a loving way. I pray you are inspired to parent with an expectation of greatness coated with understanding and patience. As a result, I pray you are able to train up your child in the way they should go, and when they are old, they will not depart from the ways of the Lord. Finally, I pray your child's heart would turn towards you in such a way that we all will witness Our Father heal our land.

MALACHI 4:6 (NKJV)

And he will turn the hearts of the fathers to the children, and the hearts of the children to their fathers, lest I come and strike the earth with a curse.

Introduction

I believe the father is the most important person in the world.

Fathers have been given a unique charge of being the head of their household and sharing the role of life-giver, protector, provider, guide, and coach in the lives of their children. Traditionally, fathers have been assigned to very specific roles in the family, like breadwinner and disciplinarian, but we've come to realize that responsible fatherhood is much more than that. Responsible fathering involves supporting children throughout their entire maturation process and, in every way necessary, ensuring they are more equipped to succeed in life than their predecessors. This call of duty includes being able to step up to the plate regardless of the parental challenges that may arise. Whether it's watching the kids, helping them learn, paying for college, or giving Mom a reprieve, fathers are an essential part of keeping the family together and training up their children to be smart working, productive, well-balanced people.

The importance of fathers is so evident that in the Scriptures, God stated if the hearts of fathers would turn towards their children, and likewise their children's hearts towards their fathers, then our nation would be spared a curse (Malachi 4:6). Unfortunately, I believe we as a society have drifted away from this central theme and, as a result, are living with the societal consequences of a curse due to the polarized hearts of fathers and children.

This critical kinship between fathers and children can be seen from more than just a Christian or religious perspective. There is a growing number of family/paternal studies that show how affectionate, supportive, and involved fathers give their children an advantage in their intellectual, verbal, and social development. It has also been proven through evidence-based research that good dads greatly contribute to their children's academic achievement, self-esteem, sense of well-being, and trustworthiness. As a result, when fathers commit to spending consistent time with their children and giving them the compassion and attention they need to properly grow in their awareness of self, everyone wins—including dad.

Another primary reason I believe the father is the most important person in the world is because it's the chief role in which God chooses to reveal Himself to us. In general, the title Father (capitalized) signifies God's role as our Creator, the ultimate Authority, and is often viewed as all-powerful and all-knowing, with a love for us that goes beyond human understanding. Throughout these lessons, you will see the different usages of "father" and "Father" to indicate a dad's relationship to their children and God's relationship to us, respectively. Ultimately, it is God the Father who loves us so much that He gave His only Son, Christ, that we may see His heart's desire for us, and in return, we would turn our hearts towards Him.

This way we will live in harmony with God as His children and reap the blessings of Him taking an active interest in our affairs. Much in the same way that a father would take an interest in his children, who are dependent on him, God responds to our humanity and takes an interest in us fulfilling our life's purpose. He acts on our behalf and ensures us that we are accepted, loved, forgiven, and treasured by Him. In essence, He offers all the security a child needs from their Father to thrive.

It is from this God's-eye view of fatherhood that I hope you see the lessons in this book. Look at them as reminders that God is all around us, in all things, caring for His children with a perfect love. Like a good father, He's with you at your highest point of potential just as much as when you're at your lowest point of failure. It's His pleasure to walk with you hand in hand through the peaks and valleys of life. In the end, He sees you as perfect—faults and all.

The goal of this book is to help you see the loving lessons God can teach fathers through their children. Specifically, the objectives of this book are to:

- **Turn your heart towards your children** — Provide inspiration and examples of how to see what God is teaching you and showing you through your children by being an engaged father.

- **Turn the hearts of your children towards you** — Win your children's admiration with compassion through your Godly example, obedience to His Word, involvement in their lives, and prayer.

- **See God as Our Father** — Plant the seed of seeing your life through the perspective of having a loving Father who cares for you.

- **Have God heal our land** — Restore the desire to have our fathers as involved leaders of the family. Restore the belonging, protection, and confidence of our children as they grow into purpose-filled lives. Experience the warmth and extension of God's love throughout our cultures that radiates from familial love and truth.

Welcome to the Fathers and Children book.

1 JOHN 3:1 (NLT)

See how very much Our Father loves us, for He calls us His children, and that is what we are!

LESSON #1

The Father Gives You Just Enough so You Remember Home

Of my two children, Johannah is not yet walking, but Jessica is, so in the mornings when I feed them breakfast, I like to keep Johannah close by my side or between my legs, and I allow Jessica to run back and forth in close proximity. As far as sheer size goes, Johannah is probably twice the size of Jessica, and this is to be expected since Johannah is going on three years old and Jessica is only approaching one. I let Jessica roam a little, because if I try to hold her down, she's going to whine, wiggle, and squiggle, which only causes more work for me, so I let her cruise the living room as we eat.

For breakfast, I tend to feed Johannah a little less than half an ounce of eggs per serving (this girl can eat, lol). but I only give Jessica about a third of that amount at any given time. The reason I give Jessica such smaller portions is not solely because of her size but also because I know if I give her too much at once, she is going to roam somewhere and stay too far away from me for too long. I'll then have to repeatedly call her, and it's only when she (1) hears her name and (2) knows that the call of her name means "more food" that she'll come running back to me. (There's something to be said about how she comes back to me only looking for more food.) So instead of giving her a lot of food at once, which would cause her to stay away from me longer, I only give her a little bit at a time. Now when she's away and hears me call her name, she'll be hungry enough to immediately come back to me.

I believe Our Father has designed us to be in constant dependence on His care in the same way. He arranges things in our lives to bring us back to Him, for us to remember that we are His, and to remind us He is our provider. If you've stepped away from God, now is a good time to turn back to Him and check in. Sometimes it takes Him putting us between a rock and a hard place for us to recognize our reliance upon Him. Other times it just takes a reminder like this lesson for you to turn back to Him and be filled.

EXODUS 16:4 (NLT)

Then the LORD said to Moses, "Look, I'm going to rain down food from heaven for you. Each day the people can go out and pick up as much food as they need for that day. I will test them in this to see whether or not they will follow My instructions."

THE FATHER GIVES YOU JUST ENOUGH SO YOU REMEMBER HOME

D	F	A	T	H	E	R	E	M	I	N	D	N	Q	Z
W	R	F	R	O	C	K	M	Z	S	E	C	Y	O	M
S	Q	Y	X	R	N	A	G	S	S	J	R	M	S	I
B	R	D	N	E	A	Z	W	I	B	D	D	L	V	O
U	M	V	E	Z	I	N	G	O	C	E	R	A	C	L
P	Q	W	D	P	L	N	G	R	O	M	Q	A	J	B
I	W	W	P	A	E	E	Z	E	N	O	U	G	H	K
R	H	N	L	D	R	N	R	B	S	H	H	X	G	S
Z	R	O	Y	Z	U	G	D	M	T	A	F	K	R	P
N	R	T	Q	M	Q	L	A	E	A	L	I	W	V	U
L	F	F	T	M	P	N	S	M	N	G	L	G	Y	N
W	W	F	Q	A	G	R	O	E	T	C	L	N	F	W
G	T	L	G	W	U	D	I	R	P	F	E	I	S	Y
U	T	W	F	B	C	T	D	B	D	U	D	W	Q	J
G	D	V	W	T	V	K	K	X	P	U	P	L	S	H

- FATHER
- DESIGNED
- CONSTANT
- DEPENDENCE
- CARE
- ARRANGES
- ENOUGH
- ROCK
- HARD
- REMIND
- RECOGNIZE
- RELIANCE
- REMEMBER
- FILLED
- HOME

LESSON #2

Trust the Father's Hands, they are Conditioned to Care for You

Throughout the day, my wife and I have to constantly moisturize both of our daughters' skin. They inherited really dry skin from me, head to toe, so we have to keep ample amounts of cream, oil, and grease products around the house. We use things like African shea butter for their skin, heavy buttercream for their hair moisturizer, and a hydrocortisone ointment for their faces because they have patches of eczema. As a family, we make it a point to stay lubed up.

Because of this, at any given time over the course of the day, I'm using my hands to care for either of my children. Since my hands have so much care on them from steady use, after I've applied lotion or sunscreen on one of my children, it's easy for me to transfer to the next child the remaining moisture that is still on my hands. This way if one of my children comes to me and they have crust on their face or a dry spot on their leg, my hands will still have enough soft residue on them that I can just wipe away the problem. As their father, I'm able to seamlessly move from one child to the next, taking care of their bumps, bruises, and dry places.

Our Father is the same way. He's been caring for His children for so long, for so many generations, that His hands are treated with the remedy to our live's issues. He's skillful in wiping away our worry, anxiety, stresses, and doubt. Our Father is the master at mending dry marriages, giving life to arid hopes, and refilling deserted dreams. With His constant involvement, there is no need for Him to re-apply His fatherly care to get His love to work for us. His love is ingrained in His touch, and when He touches us, we become whole. Trust Our Father's hand and His care for your life.

ISAIAH 64:8 (NIV)

" Yet you, LORD, are our Father. We are the clay, You are the potter; we are all the work of Your hand.

TRUST THE FATHER'S HANDS, THEY ARE CONDITIONED TO CARE FOR YOU

Z	G	E	L	D	S	T	N	A	T	S	N	O	C	M
A	Y	S	C	I	S	S	H	Q	N	N	S	U	S	S
A	K	L	I	C	E	U	Q	O	E	K	A	Q	F	D
R	Q	N	I	S	L	R	I	C	M	L	V	S	D	N
P	C	Z	T	M	M	T	A	G	E	W	O	D	N	T
R	E	F	S	N	A	R	T	D	V	D	P	H	X	Y
D	H	M	Q	R	E	F	I	L	L	I	N	G	W	M
O	F	E	E	S	S	M	M	H	O	I	J	Z	A	Q
A	S	N	I	Z	I	K	T	A	V	H	G	V	F	H
H	E	D	T	I	O	W	B	N	N	Q	Z	S	E	C
G	U	I	H	Y	Q	Z	I	D	I	G	R	G	O	Q
E	P	N	O	R	G	X	D	Q	T	O	U	C	H	R
G	A	G	U	Z	Z	Q	K	V	P	P	I	S	U	R
Y	O	C	V	J	O	T	H	X	H	T	V	U	K	G
X	B	B	Z	A	X	C	G	E	Y	Z	X	O	A	L

- FAMILY
- OINTMENT
- HAND
- CARE
- TRANSFER
- SEAMLESS
- RESIDUE
- GENERATIONS
- MENDING
- REFILLING
- CONSTANT
- INVOLVEMENT
- TOUCH
- WHOLE
- TRUST

LESSON #3

The Father's Gifts Are Intended for Specific Seasons

This is one of the earlier lessons I've learned from Our Father through my children. When my youngest girl, Jessica, was still an infant, she would want a bottle of formula every night before bedtime. Then, like clockwork, she would wake up at around 1:30 a.m. and want another four ounces of formula, so we'd hand it to her in her crib to satisfy her. After her bottle and after she'd fallen back asleep, I'd go into her room and pick up the bottle because she would sometimes leave about half an ounce in it. I didn't want this formula staying out all night because she could possibly end up drinking it in the morning.

But sometimes I forget to go back in the room and pick up the bottle, so it's still there in the morning when we bring her a new bottle for breakfast. At this point, we've already taken Jessica out of her crib, and she's not too concerned with the overnight bottle, because she's playing. But when I'm getting my older daughter dressed, Jessica will sometimes look over and see that the old bottle still has half an ounce in it, and she wants to finish it off. When she grabs the overnight bottle and attempts to drink it, I quickly snatch it out of her hand and won't give it back to her. This causes her to immediately get angry with me because she knows this is something that is good, and I'm preventing her from having it. She's well aware that the formula is nourishing, that it is a daily part of her life, and that it is something I would normally freely give to her without hesitation. But because the formula was not immediately used in the intended state it was given and could potentially harm her in its expired state, it's my duty as a caring father to snatch it out of her hand and not allow her to drink it.

Isn't this just like Our Father? There are things that God may have given us in one season of life that may not be good for us in another. We have to trust Him more than we trust our familiarity and comfort. A wise man once told me if you eat an apple that's rotten or out of season, it can almost kill you, but an apple in season is very tasty and healthy. We have to learn to trust Our Father's timing, purpose, and prohibitions for us through our various seasons of life.

ECCLESIASTES 3:1 (NLT)

 For everything there is a season, a time for every activity under heaven.

THE FATHER'S GIFTS ARE INTENDED FOR SPECIFIC SEASONS

Y	G	B	C	T	M	B	M	O	J	A	J	Y	B	O
B	B	M	Z	F	S	P	E	F	V	F	G	S	T	C
S	I	Z	P	O	G	U	I	R	D	I	Q	T	Q	O
Z	W	U	Z	R	N	A	R	O	E	U	C	R	H	M
V	O	J	D	M	I	O	W	T	D	A	E	E	T	F
P	K	T	Q	U	M	O	V	T	N	P	A	B	A	O
W	I	U	Q	L	I	G	C	E	E	L	E	M	S	R
K	K	C	P	A	T	I	E	N	T	N	I	E	Q	T
M	V	W	J	B	U	W	T	H	N	L	A	N	E	V
P	Q	H	Y	L	A	A	Y	R	I	S	J	E	S	M
N	Z	N	A	D	N	K	R	A	O	T	B	R	O	V
A	Z	V	M	C	O	C	R	N	H	L	M	D	P	V
Q	I	U	E	L	B	I	S	N	O	P	S	E	R	S
D	U	S	C	T	T	W	Y	H	P	I	Z	S	U	Z
W	O	F	U	Y	R	V	L	D	W	R	U	Z	P	P

- TIMING
- PURPOSE
- REMEMBER
- TRUST
- SEASONS
- ROTTEN
- HEALTHY
- INTENDED
- COMFORT
- FAMILIARITY
- WISDOM
- PATIENT
- RESPONSIBLE
- FORMULA
- REPENTANCE

LESSON #4

Children Are a Reflection of Their Father's Love

There are times when I hold my children and look them in their eyes, and when they look back into mine, they look at me in such a way that I feel like they see themselves within me. By seeing themselves in me, I mean they see how and where they got their look, how they determine what is funny, where they learned to laugh, how they develop their worth, and from where they will grow into their identity. When I peer into their innocent and optimistic eyes, I can see them wanting to be like me in their future. I can see them weighing the possibilities of what they will be able to do and who they can become.

In the same way, when we're locked in our gaze, I see myself in them. I see my future, I see all of my hopes, and I see the best of what I have to offer in life. I see new possibilities to explore, I see beauty, and I see a newness of who I am and who I will become. This two-way devotion is our father–child love mirror. It reflects how and where we are one. Through the mirror, I take in all of who my children are, and they look into their father for all they can possibly be. In these moments, it becomes apparent how much we are really one. They are me, and I am them. To know either one of us is to know the building blocks of the other. There is nothing that can separate us!

I believe Our Father created a Father–child love mirror of His own when He spoke us into existence. By saying, "Let Us make mankind in Our image, and in Our likeness" (Gen. 1:26, NKJV), He reveals His never-ending desire to see Himself through our lives. As His children, Our Father sees how His love takes form and fulfills His dreams of mirroring His heavenly kingdom here on earth. When we live by His Spirit, we embody the change He desires to see in the world. Let's embrace our identity and exercise the connection we have as extensions of the King. Let's look to Him and fully grasp our grandeur of potential to reflect Our Father's creative, spiritual, intelligent, communicative, relational, moral, and purposeful characteristics. After all, we are a reflection of His love, and it's in His love that we see who we really are.

JOHN 17:20–23 (NIV)

" My prayer is not for them alone. I pray also for those who will believe in Me through their message, that all of them may be one, Father, just as You are in Me and I am in You. May they also be in Us so that the world may believe that You have sent Me. I have given them the glory that You gave Me, that they may be one as We are One—I in them and You in Me—so that they may be brought to complete unity. Then the world will know that You sent Me and have loved them even as You have loved Me.

CHILDREN ARE A REFLECTION OF THEIR FATHER'S LOVE

G	U	O	S	V	A	F	D	S	C	I	T	F	G	K
D	W	M	D	W	D	T	L	I	A	R	U	G	Z	S
E	K	S	Z	P	N	F	T	D	J	T	U	S	E	W
Z	A	T	V	W	O	S	I	Y	U	O	A	R	O	O
T	J	W	Q	Z	I	T	D	R	R	G	R	M	R	R
A	G	G	Y	M	T	T	E	S	G	D	W	T	O	T
A	N	O	I	T	C	E	N	N	O	C	H	R	H	H
V	E	T	F	W	E	H	T	L	T	C	R	X	Y	I
P	P	S	K	Q	L	Y	I	E	R	I	S	E	D	O
O	X	T	I	A	F	K	T	G	M	K	A	Q	O	N
R	S	F	K	C	E	N	Y	I	B	B	Y	L	B	B
D	P	L	N	N	R	U	E	D	N	A	R	G	M	B
B	N	F	E	R	R	E	M	W	C	U	J	A	E	V
A	M	S	Z	X	H	K	X	C	C	I	Q	U	C	F
R	S	Y	X	V	D	O	H	E	L	H	I	O	H	E

- WORTH
- IDENTITY
- OPTIMISTIC
- FUTURE
- MIRROR
- LIKENESS
- DESIRE
- EMBODY
- EMBRACE
- EXERCISE
- CONNECTION
- GRANDEUR
- POTENTIAL
- REFLECTION
- UNITY

LESSON #5

Obedience to the Father Comes With Liberty

Jessica is getting really tall and active. I like seeing her explore her surroundings. It shows me that she's growing up properly, and I cherish that it's happening right before my eyes; she is such a happy baby. Now that she's aware of her newfound height, she pulls up to stand on a lot of stuff around the house. Overall, this is great as it shows me her strength and agility, but on the other hand, I don't understand why she has the tendency to pull up on the trash can. Of all the things to play with around the house, she'll go straight for the kitchen trash can, pull off the lid, take out different pieces of trash, and either play with them or try to eat them, which, either way, is totally disgusting.

Considering we have a house full of furniture to stand up against, not to mention all of the other things that she can play with or chew on around the house that's permissible, the trash can is something that is off limits to her, and I repeatedly tell her, "Don't touch." As with most kids, she'll follow my instruction for a little while, but lately she's been back to pulling up and pulling out trash. So now, as a reminder of what I've forbidden her to do, she gets a pop on her finger. Popping her finger is not something I want to do nor does it bring me any satisfaction, but since she has a problem obeying my commands, this is something necessary for her to understand boundaries. Bottom line for her, the trashcan is not to be touched. As soon as I see her touch it, I say something like, "Do not touch this trashcan, and the day you touch this trashcan is the day your finger is going to get popped!"

I believe it is this type of responsible fathering Our Father shows us in His Word when He gave clear instructions to Adam to not eat from the tree of the knowledge of good and evil (but he did).

I can also look back into my own life and remember the many times when God nudged me to obey Him but I found my own ideas to be more pleasing. I would disobey Him, and He would pursue me by shutting down opportunities in my life that would have continually led me further away from His desire for me. He loves us too much to let us disobey Him, so sometimes He pops our finger, other times He dries up a relationship, and when needed, He'll put an angel on duty to stop us by any means necessary.

GENESIS 3:24 (NLT)

 After sending them out, the LORD God stationed mighty cherubim to the east of the Garden of Eden. And he placed a flaming sword that flashed back and forth to guard the way to the tree of life.

OBEDIENCE TO THE FATHER COMES WITH LIBERTY

F	G	H	Q	D	L	W	R	V	U	C	C	P	I	I
U	N	R	O	O	P	P	O	R	T	U	N	I	T	Y
A	B	O	U	N	D	A	R	I	E	S	I	H	O	A
F	G	A	I	W	J	V	H	L	R	C	D	S	A	H
E	D	N	A	T	S	R	E	D	N	U	T	N	C	S
Q	I	A	G	C	C	P	G	K	T	H	Q	O	V	Y
E	R	A	C	S	X	U	M	Y	O	L	M	I	L	W
N	B	E	H	N	L	B	R	V	O	M	H	T	I	M
C	Y	X	E	N	F	B	E	T	A	R	H	A	B	F
M	I	O	R	E	S	P	O	N	S	I	S	L	E	T
D	W	X	U	O	B	E	D	I	E	N	C	E	R	D
X	X	Q	B	P	Y	S	X	U	V	F	I	R	T	Y
P	E	F	I	N	G	E	R	S	I	I	I	D	Y	L
N	L	M	M	M	C	R	G	F	L	F	U	T	W	R
W	T	I	S	B	T	S	L	N	R	J	L	X	S	N

- BENEFITS
- BOUNDARIES
- OBEDIENCE
- RESPONSIBLE
- OPPORTUNITY
- RELATIONSHIP
- COMMANDS
- INSTRUCTION
- LIBERTY
- CHERUBIM
- UNDERSTAND
- GOOD
- EVIL
- DUTY
- FINGER

LESSON #6

The Father Reminds Us It's Going to Be Okay

When Johannah was younger, she used to have seizures, and when she would seize, I would feel very confused, helpless, at times hopeless, and emotionally distraught. I'd feel this way because I did not know how to stop the seizures, and after many attempts, we still couldn't find the right medication nor did we know of anything or anyone who knew how to stop my baby girl from shaking. So each day, multiple times a day, month over month for almost a year, she would seize, and we sought the best experts in the field to help cure her. Our pursuits only led to more tests and trials and to the next recommendation. It was during this time I would pray for a miracle or an answer, and God would tell me, "Do not worry about Johannah. She is already healed; I have her in My plans." Although I heard Him, I still couldn't see any difference in her condition. Everything my wife and I experienced on the outside looked the same, and to a degree, things looked like they were getting worse because time kept passing and the seizures kept occurring.

But every now and then, when I was scared, when I was at my max of what I could hold as a father, I'd have my daughter in my arms while she was seizing, and at the end of her seizure, she would just look at me and smile. Not just any smile either—she would render a generous ear-to-ear grin as if to say, "Hey, Dad, I'm still here, and I'm okay." Looking at her, I couldn't help but smile with her even though on the inside of me everything was falling apart. Her smile in the middle of this heart-breaking moment would remind me of Our Father's promise to me, and so I would do my best to be present and enjoy the moment with her.

Those moments came to mind during our annual family trip to New Orleans. We've made it a tradition to go visit my wife's side of the family, and on our way back this year, we had bad turbulence. This turbulence caused a heightened level of panic in the plane, but one of the senses that really stimulates Johannah is called "vestibular" (which is how we know our spatial recognition, a.k.a. the stuff you feel on roller coasters), and Johannah really loves this type of sensory input. So while everyone else was freaking out, concerned about the heavy turbulence, I turned to look at Johannah, and again she was smiling. She was smiling, she was laughing, and she was having a ball.

Our Father then reminded me that though our world may be falling apart and everyone around us is losing their heads with no clue how to stop the decline, He says since He has you in His plans, you can smile.

PSALM 16:11 (NLT)

" You will show me the way of life, granting me the joy of Your presence and the pleasures of living with You forever.

THE FATHER REMINDS US IT'S GOING TO BE OKAY

U	Z	E	F	L	A	Y	C	F	N	E	E	W	R	P
V	R	H	Y	W	W	D	O	F	N	C	L	N	R	S
G	C	V	P	Q	I	P	N	I	N	N	V	I	L	L
T	M	E	L	O	N	B	D	E	D	E	Z	W	M	R
Q	E	T	A	L	U	M	I	T	S	L	P	T	X	S
J	P	O	N	K	O	T	T	T	S	U	R	T	E	F
I	L	U	S	H	A	K	I	N	G	B	V	I	T	N
U	I	B	K	P	Q	B	O	O	M	R	Z	H	B	H
K	F	E	G	N	U	W	N	J	M	U	Q	L	J	V
Y	V	P	Q	L	W	O	E	D	R	T	W	I	O	A
I	W	V	A	E	A	G	Q	E	Y	O	H	T	I	R
P	L	R	Q	T	F	P	M	N	F	I	T	G	U	N
U	H	C	F	W	H	I	B	J	N	K	K	E	Y	Z
N	X	S	U	W	N	N	L	O	F	N	G	V	B	C
K	C	K	W	D	T	G	O	Y	A	K	O	X	T	H

- TURBULENCE
- SMILE
- PLANS
- VESTIBULAR
- SHAKING
- PATH
- LIFE
- ENJOY
- PATIENCE
- TRUST
- CONDITION
- REMIND
- SEIZURE
- STIMULATE
- OKAY

LESSON #7

The Father Knows What You Can Handle

As I'm getting dressed in the morning and preparing my girls for the day, quite often I feed them breakfast. Depending on how early I drop them off at school or daycare, they may be able to have breakfast there, but if I drop them off after 8 a.m., I like to have fed them something before leaving the house. I feed them because ultimately I don't know what the daycare people are going to do once I drop them off. I know the staff at daycare are good people, and I trust they will ensure proper care of their students, but I don't want to put my daughters in a situation where they're hungry and not being fed at daycare because of an assumption they're being fed at home or vice versa.

As long as they are in my hands, I do all I can to get them ready for a successful day. So when I'm feeding them in the morning (I typically make eggs. I hook 'em up too; Dad knows how to hook up some eggs btw), I have Johannah and Jessica both between my legs, and if I can, I have them facing each other while also facing me to let them know this is daddy/daughter breakfast time. To be honest, I really make the eggs for Johannah, but whenever I feed Johannah something, Jessica comes around and wants whatever her big sister has, so I end up feeding them both.

Since the eggs are primarily for Johannah, because Jessica eats organic baby food, I give her the larger portion of the eggs. I'd say they eat about five eggs total. Johannah eats almost a half ounce scoop at a time, and Jessica gets about half of that per spoonful. When I'm toggling the scoops, I can see Jessica looking to see how much I give Johannah and slowly noticing how she isn't getting as much as her sister. The problem with Jessica comparing portion sizes with her sister is that she can't handle what I give Johannah. If I were to give Jessica what she's asking for, she'd probably choke. So I give her what she can handle.

A good father gives his child what they can handle even though it may be different than what another one of his children can manage. Conversely, Johannah will see me feed Jessica more often because when Johannah is still chewing on her larger portion of eggs, I give Jessica another of her smaller spoonfuls. This causes Johannah to open her mouth to suggest "it's my turn in the feeding toggle," but when she opens her mouth, I still see the eggs I gave her before, so I say, "No, no, no…finish what I've given you first; then I'll give you more".

I believe Our Father also demonstrates this level of attentiveness with us as an extension of His provision, protection, and wisdom. He understands our needs regardless of what we may or may not want and fills us to the measure we can responsibly sustain. Our Father knows what we can handle, and He also can determine if what we're currently working on fills up our plate. As such, He knows when it's time for us to be trusted with an increase or if it's time for us to first finish the work He's already given us.

LUKE 11:11–13 (NLT)

> You fathers—if your children ask for a fish, do you give them a snake instead? Or if they ask for an egg, do you give them a scorpion? Of course not! So if you sinful people know how to give good gifts to your children, how much more will your heavenly Father give the Holy Spirit to those who ask Him.

THE FATHER KNOWS WHAT YOU CAN HANDLE

M	F	K	O	C	U	Q	I	P	E	F	V	V	M	F
Y	F	M	E	R	M	K	V	M	S	N	D	Y	M	I
U	S	E	S	S	E	C	C	U	S	V	W	B	Y	W
N	K	H	G	W	S	G	O	Z	Q	D	Z	P	O	H
D	D	T	A	A	P	C	A	M	P	G	F	R	O	B
E	V	N	A	B	X	O	N	R	F	D	G	O	W	L
R	T	R	B	Y	I	P	O	Z	D	N	J	C	N	B
S	N	O	I	T	A	T	I	M	I	L	P	E	H	V
T	Z	Z	L	I	E	N	S	G	R	E	E	S	K	A
A	U	E	I	C	S	X	I	F	R	D	A	S	X	J
N	X	A	T	A	C	L	V	S	S	U	B	E	S	X
D	U	I	I	P	E	R	O	T	F	L	Q	E	D	P
I	O	S	E	A	P	N	R	G	O	G	X	V	L	T
N	D	D	S	C	A	U	P	T	Q	P	Q	A	U	G
G	Q	H	G	L	H	L	L	Z	I	Z	B	V	T	B

- PERSONAL
- PROCESS
- PROVISION
- PROTECTION
- UNDERSTANDING
- NEEDS
- REGARDLESS
- HURTS
- HABITS
- WANTS
- ABILITIES
- LIMITATIONS
- GROW
- CAPACITY
- SUCCESSES

LESSON #8

The Father's Children Know His Voice

My littlest girl Jessica is very curious. Everytime she sees me nearby doing anything interesting, it becomes her mission to know exactly what's going on with me. Even when she hears me around a corner she'll slowly come crawling, bit by bit, to see how she can best supervise my activities. But before she was old enough to crawl throughout the house, she'd make do with randomly bobbing her head in a jumper or staring at me while propped up in a baby chair.

Soon a pattern became clear to me that as soon as she didn't see me in her immediate line of sight, she'd begin to cry. To try to get around this behavior, I started experimenting with various ways to help her understand that even though she doesn't always see me, I'm still here. To train her trust that her father has never left her, I would first talk to her while I'm in her presence then gradually turn a corner, out of her sight, while continuing the same conversation so she could recognize the continuity. I'd say things in my friendliest vocal tones like, "Hey…Dad's still here…I know you hear me…" and I would see her eyes searching and her mind racing to try to make sense of hearing my voice without seeing my face. After a while she'd get frustrated and begin to cry, so I would return into her presence. I would repeat this routine to see how long I could go without being physically present with her while she still remained comforted by her father's words.

This reminds me of how Our Father continues to stretch our faith in His Word and build our confidence in Him that He is always with us, regardless if we see or feel Him or not. It is in our maturity that we understand He is no less closer to us when we're deep in a struggle with our secret sin than when we're in our most heartfelt worship service. Our faith requires us to trust His words and find comfort in His voice even when we're uncertain where He is or when we are feeling helpless and alone. As our heavenly Father, He will never leave us, and there is nothing that can ever separate us from His love. That's what His Word says. Let's trust it.

JOHN 10:3–5 (NIV)

" The gatekeeper opens the gate for Him, and the sheep listen to His voice. He calls His own sheep by name and leads them out. When He has brought out all His own, He goes on ahead of them, and His sheep follow Him because they know His voice. But they will never follow a stranger; in fact, they will run away from him because they do not recognize a stranger's voice.

THE FATHER'S CHILDREN KNOW HIS VOICE

W	W	S	A	J	M	S	M	N	K	Z	C	B	V	O
P	K	Z	E	A	Q	P	W	S	G	O	W	X	X	J
S	P	P	J	T	E	Q	E	C	N	E	S	E	R	P
H	U	B	P	E	C	I	O	V	I	R	S	J	C	G
B	K	O	H	T	S	H	E	P	H	E	R	D	E	Q
P	C	S	I	A	T	R	U	S	T	I	N	E	V	J
X	A	X	Q	R	S	Q	E	V	O	L	B	S	Q	X
Y	N	T	L	A	U	I	G	W	N	A	Y	P	O	F
A	X	H	T	P	F	C	P	O	F	Q	U	V	C	K
W	O	I	J	E	Z	F	O	S	L	R	B	C	W	S
Z	O	G	T	S	R	K	I	M	C	W	M	Y	X	X
N	J	R	T	Q	M	N	J	Q	F	M	S	P	M	O
U	Q	O	D	X	D	W	O	L	L	O	F	U	B	W
H	L	W	L	S	R	S	H	H	G	O	R	K	G	P
A	S	N	J	H	L	B	Z	F	V	P	L	T	Q	G

- CURIOUS
- PATTERN
- TRUST
- PRESENCE
- VOICE
- SHEEP
- COMFORT
- CONVERSATION
- SHEPHERD
- FOLLOW
- NOTHING
- CAN
- SEPARATE
- LOVE
- WORD

LESSON #9

When the Father Calls, Where Are You?

Sometimes when I see Johannah doing something she shouldn't do, even when she doesn't know where I am, I'll call out her name. Calling her name in this way doesn't mean I want her to come to me. Instead, it's me making her aware of what she's currently doing so that she will consider if she should continue doing it. So it goes like this: I'll pass by a room and see her sucking her thumb or pounding on a closet door, and I'll call, "Johannah…?!" and without delay, she'll look around and decide if what she's doing is right or wrong and make the proper corrections if necessary.

It is my intent that when she hears me call her name she knows I am nearby and that she is seen and accounted for. My cue is a sign of my love that conveys, "Now that you know I see you doing whatever you're doing, whether good or bad, you now have time to continue or adjust that behavior." Ultimately, she knows my call for her awareness and correction precedes my power, authority, and the possible penalty that will follow if she continues any misbehavior. Since she is so young, it is not my preference to lead with an iron fist but rather to have her understand my heart, my tone, and the reasons behind my inquisitions.

As such, I think Our Father sometimes calls our attention towards Him, not because He doesn't know where we are, as seen when He said to Adam, "Where are you?" after they had sinned in the Garden of Eden but so we can take His prompting as a time to look around and gather our thoughts on what we're doing and where we are and make the necessary corrections. I believe our Father calls us to speak to our location. He calls us to speak to the state of our hearts. He calls us to remember our love and trust we have with each other. He calls our names to give us a few moments and opportunities to right any wrongs we may have committed. Take this opportunity and spend a few moments considering where you are in life, the state of your heart, the condition of your relationships, and any wrongs that you may have committed. Speak to Our Father. He's listening.

GENESIS 3:8–9 (NLT)

" When the cool evening breezes were blowing, the man and his wife heard the LORD God walking about in the garden. So they hid from the LORD God among the trees. Then the LORD God called to the man, "Where are you?"

WHEN THE FATHER CALLS, WHERE ARE YOU?

O	V	Z	K	R	W	E	J	P	Z	C	C	I	I	W
L	L	R	X	Q	J	V	D	A	A	N	Y	X	O	M
Y	R	E	M	E	M	B	E	R	V	O	L	E	S	E
Z	E	T	A	T	A	T	A	K	C	N	Y	J	E	Q
Y	L	U	D	W	Y	S	L	J	Y	A	Q	L	S	L
M	A	S	A	I	A	U	G	R	D	R	Z	W	U	T
Y	T	I	N	U	T	R	O	P	P	O	G	E	X	L
R	I	N	T	E	N	T	E	F	K	E	V	O	A	P
E	O	Z	L	W	N	D	W	X	X	C	S	C	L	H
H	N	I	O	E	I	E	W	N	U	S	G	T	B	Z
T	S	L	V	C	I	Z	D	R	I	B	B	C	P	C
A	H	N	E	A	R	B	Y	E	W	F	U	A	S	A
F	I	D	O	H	H	J	A	B	T	E	W	Q	T	L
R	P	U	T	R	A	E	H	A	X	Y	J	F	P	I
D	S	N	Z	P	B	G	Z	O	R	X	Y	H	Y	H

- FATHER
- ADAM
- NEARBY
- INTENT
- AWARE
- DECIDE
- INVENTORY
- OPPORTUNITY
- REMEMBER
- LOVE
- TRUST
- HEART
- RELATIONSHIPS
- BEHAVIOR
- EDEN

LESSON #10

You Are in the Father's Plans, Faults and All

It was early in the morning, my girls had been awake since 6:30 a.m., and we are well into our morning routine. They were already dressed, their bags were packed and ready to go to school, and it was only a little past 8 a.m. Since Johannah has physical therapy at 9 a.m., I was hoping to get out the door and drop Jessica off at daycare on my way to Johannah's session. Yes!

While getting them dressed, I noticed that Jessica was full of energy and curiosity, so she was getting into things around the house that she shouldn't tamper with. She was standing on her tippy toes to open drawers, climbing up the bookcase shelves, playing with the toilet, crawling into the bathtub, and other random acts while I was trying to get her sister dressed and keep a watchful eye on her. All this activity caused me to stop dressing Johannah, find Jessica and put her in a safe place, give her something distracting to play with, pacify her whining, and juggle our morning schedule commitments with keeping her out of trouble.

Then it dawned on me that as much as Jessica may be doing things she is not allowed to do, making mistakes along the way, and doing things "wrong" (also paying those consequences), in my father's love for her, her wrongs are embraced with the same care as I embrace her. I see her inquisitive trials, playful failures, and first time successes as parts of her learning process. She may continue to mess up and continually get it wrong, but that's when I continually correct, continually guide, continually instruct, continually pull her closer to me, and continually give her opportunities to get it right. As long as she's my child and she's growing within my grace, even when she messes up, she's exactly where I want her to be.

Our Father's compassion is the same way towards us. As His children, there is nothing that we can do to end His love towards us. The beautiful thing about it all is that He loves us and He knows us through and through. He loves us in spite of our odd pet peeves just as much as He does while knowing our swagger. He's not caught off guard by our disobedience, and He knows the things we struggle with most. Yet He chooses to continually show us patience, grace, and mercy in our journey to become better men. I pray we know His Fatherly embrace and live in the grace of His forgiveness and in the liberty of His acceptance.

PSALM 103:8–14 (NLT)

> The LORD is compassionate and merciful, slow to get angry and filled with unfailing love. He will not constantly accuse us, nor remain angry forever. He does not punish us for all our sins; He does not deal harshly with us, as we deserve. For His unfailing love toward those who fear Him is as great as the height of the heavens above the earth. He has removed our sins as far from us as the east is from the west. The LORD is like a Father to His children, tender and compassionate to those who fear Him. For He knows how weak we are; He remembers we are only dust.

YOU ARE IN THE FATHER'S PLANS, FAULTS AND ALL

N	Q	I	L	U	D	X	J	F	Y	R	E	K	T	W
O	E	I	J	N	K	X	F	T	C	G	N	Y	E	U
H	N	L	I	N	P	C	R	H	R	B	I	H	N	W
C	C	E	B	X	Z	E	E	A	E	B	H	O	D	R
Y	L	A	D	Y	B	F	C	S	M	G	I	I	E	H
F	O	R	G	I	V	E	N	E	S	S	T	G	R	V
V	S	N	L	N	U	C	A	K	S	T	G	A	G	F
O	E	I	F	S	X	G	T	A	Z	A	I	A	I	C
Y	R	N	M	T	G	E	P	T	W	U	X	B	S	C
W	H	G	Q	R	T	M	E	S	C	B	P	K	U	I
D	Y	U	V	U	O	B	C	I	I	E	T	K	U	B
Q	V	U	S	C	C	R	C	M	R	V	R	Z	L	I
A	H	A	B	T	L	A	A	H	Q	X	E	R	L	E
K	R	I	R	T	H	C	R	L	I	D	Y	Q	O	D
C	D	S	U	I	V	E	S	U	Q	I	F	Q	K	C

- EMBRACE
- ACCEPTANCE
- LIBERTY
- FORGIVENESS
- SWAGGER
- COMPASSION
- CORRECT
- GUIDE
- INSTRUCT
- TENDER
- MISTAKES
- LEARNING
- CLOSER
- GRACE
- MERCY

LESSON #11

The Father Writes Down His Love for You

Fatherhood has taught me so much about our heavenly Father; I'm truly humbled by His care for me. My youngest child Jessica is pulling up, climbing over, and getting into everything around the house these days. Recently I saw her reaching into the bottom half of the oven; the fact that she now knows how to open the door to the broiler is trouble (thank God it was off and cool) because firstly she's not permitted near the oven and secondly there are all kinds of grimy, greasy, icky stuff in there that's not safe to fiddle with. Witnessing her do this, I tried to "reason" with her about her misbehavior, so I asked her a series of questions: "What are you doing?" "You know you're not allowed to touch that, right?" then out of curiosity, "Do you even *know* you're not allowed to do that?" Lastly I reminded her, "I've told you before not to touch that." I know she's only nine months old and doesn't really understand me, but I like to talk to her like she does so I can help push her to where she needs to be in her speech and vocabulary development.

The thinking behind my questions showed me how a just father could only hold his children accountable for the actions he's actually told them to do or not to do. Further, given a child's memory, once they've been told what's expected of them, it's highly probable that over time they may quickly forget their father's instructions. So when the father asks, "Do you *know* you aren't supposed to do that?" and the child's response is "No," their disobedience may not be because they weren't told but because they've genuinely forgotten. In some cases, there may be room for the child to think they're being held accountable for something they "didn't know" they shouldn't do. So then what could a responsible father do? He could say, "Okay, I'll write my instructions down in a real loving way so if you ever forget what I've said, you can always find out what I expect from you."

By the way, I will only tell Jessica to do or not do things that will bless her life because I love her deeply, and I only want the best for her. I have great plans for her, and my rules are strategically designed to give her a great shot at a bright and fulfilling future. Practically, I know she routinely puts her thumb in her mouth, so having her hands in that cruddy part of the oven may potentially make her sick or cause greater harm.

This helps me see God's Word in a new light, one that is not focused merely on rigid rules for the sake of policing but as a means to communicate with us in a way that we can rely upon. We can always go back to see what He said and try to understand it through the life and character of His Son, who lived it out as an example for us to follow. I'm thankful that Our Father didn't hide His instructions and leave us to live a life of punishing landmines, but rather He penned a Book of love, sacrifice, obedience, and power for us to read and find comfort in His fatherly protection.

2 TIMOTHY 3:16–17 (NLT)

> All Scripture is inspired by God and is useful to teach us what is true and to make us realize what is wrong in our lives. It corrects us when we are wrong and teaches us to do what is right. God uses it to prepare and equip his people to do every good work.

THE FATHER WRITES DOWN HIS LOVE FOR YOU

S	N	N	B	N	B	A	T	N	F	D	U	D	C	I
C	N	R	T	F	A	T	H	E	R	H	O	O	D	X
D	W	O	N	K	M	W	C	D	C	O	M	D	K	T
V	O	N	I	B	G	H	K	U	G	M	N	F	C	F
X	R	J	G	T	Z	F	X	Q	U	A	A	O	T	U
E	K	E	A	C	C	O	U	N	T	A	B	L	E	A
Q	L	J	T	M	L	U	I	S	A	S	G	Z	I	L
L	L	B	U	C	R	C	R	I	C	Z	D	Y	R	C
I	S	I	A	O	A	E	E	T	A	E	X	O	S	A
W	H	T	G	T	D	R	B	L	S	Y	R	E	V	E
G	G	W	E	N	I	M	A	M	M	N	O	B	Q	S
U	X	P	U	Q	M	F	V	H	E	B	I	U	W	K
K	O	V	F	G	O	M	O	V	C	M	I	D	D	K
G	M	E	D	R	O	I	E	R	A	P	E	R	P	V
M	N	K	Z	C	E	X	A	M	P	L	E	R	X	D

- FATHERHOOD
- ACCOUNTABLE
- KNOW
- REMEMBER
- UNDERSTAND
- COMMUNICATE
- CHARACTER
- PREPARE
- EQUIP
- PROFITABLE
- EVERY
- GOOD
- WORK
- INSTRUCTIONS
- EXAMPLE

LESSON #12

Testing the Father's Limits

In the process of training Johannah to not suck her thumb, I noticed that if I'm close enough to her and I raise my hand, which means stop, she'll perk up and pop her thumb right out of her mouth. She does this quickly and with urgency because she knows she should not be sucking her thumb in the first place. On the other hand, I also noticed that the farther I am away from her, I can see her contemplating and making some sort of assessment to see whether or not I can penalize her from the distance I am from her. Occasionally she'll determine in her little bitty mind that I can't reach her from where I am, so she'll continue to suck her thumb while simultaneously keeping an eye on me in case I come any closer.

To make things even more interesting, when I do get up and move closer to her, she gradually pulls her hand out of her mouth, but if I sit back down, she'll resume with sucking her thumb again. You gotta be kidding me! This cat and mouse game of hers caused me to question, "Why is she trying to gauge if I'm close enough to enforce a penalty or not? And why is she only willing to obey my command to the degree that I am able to penalize her?" Subsequently, if she determines I'm at a distance where I cannot be effective, then she will continue to do what it is she knows she is not supposed to do.

How often do we treat Our Father like He's not omnipresent, as if He's not everywhere at the same time, and continue to behave in ways in which we only conditionally obey? It seems in our times of devotion is where we sincerely seek to please the Father, but in times of frustration or trial, we'd rather He not meddle with our bad habits. We should strive to move past tip-toeing the line of what He's commanded us not to do and move closer to desiring to live the blessed life of obeying Him wholeheartedly. Our Father doesn't desire to continually police our behavior by penalty, but rather He wants to lovingly mature us in obedience to live liberated, purpose-driven lives.

PSALM 139:7–10 (NLT)

" I can never escape from Your Spirit! I can never get away from Your presence! If I go up to heaven, You are there; if I go down to the grave, You are there. If I ride the wings of the morning, if I dwell by the farthest oceans, even there Your hand will guide me, and Your strength will support me.

TESTING THE FATHER'S LIMITS

O	E	G	L	X	O	Y	G	N	B	H	B	S	S	V
M	W	L	O	S	M	T	N	Y	T	S	I	B	S	P
J	X	B	Q	H	N	L	I	G	K	M	T	U	E	L
R	E	L	A	T	I	O	N	S	H	I	P	S	C	W
Z	T	N	Y	U	P	E	I	N	J	P	E	O	C	B
U	D	T	I	I	R	M	A	T	O	D	R	U	U	A
I	L	B	S	T	E	Y	R	R	I	E	S	G	S	T
T	C	I	S	D	S	F	T	W	M	D	O	X	W	T
N	Z	P	M	B	E	N	J	O	Y	I	N	G	O	I
J	P	P	I	I	N	E	B	O	V	U	A	O	X	C
O	T	R	U	S	T	I	N	G	R	G	L	V	C	D
K	N	A	K	H	Q	S	F	K	H	R	B	E	H	B
C	Y	E	N	W	L	R	J	R	C	Q	V	K	W	W
Y	R	F	L	K	U	F	B	X	H	U	C	Q	X	C
A	L	W	C	P	K	G	L	J	F	Y	H	G	F	Y

- OMNIPRESENT
- PERSONAL
- NEEDS
- CONDITIONS
- LIMITS
- FEAR
- TRAINING
- TRUSTING
- ENJOYING
- RELATIONSHIP
- GUIDE
- STRENGTH
- SUPPORT
- SUCCESS
- HAND

LESSON #13

The Father Can Handle Your Anger

Sometimes when Johannah gets in trouble—and it's not like she gets in trouble a lot—she turns her back towards me because she doesn't want to see me anymore. I guess in turning around, she thinks for a moment that she doesn't have to deal with me or be reminded of the trouble she's in, or maybe it's her way of giving me the silent treatment. But even while her back is to me, I still continue to talk to her (in a loving way), and I can see by her ear movement, facial expressions, and body language that she still hears me. As a father who's in it for the long haul, this is okay with me. I can handle her turning her back to me for a little while because she's angry. That doesn't offend me, because I know it's a part of her understanding process.

I know she is still learning how to express herself; I know we all get frustrated at times, and when we don't get what we want, we tend to cope in ways we think benefit us. I know over time these small rubs will fade, but our bond as father and child will continue for a lifetime, so as long as I know she hears me in her anger, I give her space to reconcile her emotions.

Personally, I can really relate to getting in trouble because I don't always do things correctly, especially when it comes to doing what I should do in obedience to God. For this reason, lessons about getting in trouble tend to stick out more easily and more frequently to me. I thank God He is a Father who can handle my anger towards Him when I don't think He knows what He's doing or He is not doing it on my terms. We should be thankful that Our Father knows this world is full of frustration and pain; therefore He understands that we get angry at times. But even when we don't trust His control or when we think He's done something wrong (which He never does), let's be mindful to remain within speaking and listening distance to Him so that even while we are ticked off, He can still comfort us with His words and presence.

JONAH 3:10–4:1 (NLT)

"When God saw what they had done and how they had put a stop to their evil ways, He changed His mind and did not carry out the destruction He had threatened. This change of plans greatly upset Jonah, and he became very angry.

THE FATHER CAN HANDLE YOUR ANGER

J	J	H	R	F	W	R	U	E	K	G	Z	C	E	U
W	W	L	J	H	O	R	R	T	A	W	S	L	J	O
M	G	R	X	W	D	E	E	D	Z	L	J	O	M	O
G	R	W	G	M	M	H	I	E	J	N	Q	S	H	D
X	E	C	N	A	T	S	I	D	O	U	Y	E	I	F
M	G	N	I	N	E	T	S	I	L	B	V	V	X	D
V	N	N	K	Y	F	A	T	H	E	R	H	O	O	D
N	A	M	A	M	C	A	V	N	E	W	A	R	X	M
P	Q	R	E	R	R	A	E	V	Z	U	H	P	T	Y
W	A	O	P	T	B	F	G	S	A	F	Q	M	C	I
O	D	I	S	C	I	P	L	I	N	E	T	I	H	L
F	Y	U	U	T	R	O	U	B	L	E	A	R	N	I
U	R	V	S	M	W	F	N	Y	H	O	H	I	L	U
F	T	G	Z	A	I	L	S	E	G	Y	X	X	J	U
V	S	L	S	D	Z	B	P	M	F	B	V	K	W	B

- TROUBLE
- SLOW
- ANGER
- FRUSTRATION
- REMAIN

- CLOSE
- SPEAKING
- LISTENING
- DISTANCE
- LEARN

- UNIQUE
- DISCIPLINE
- BENEFITS
- IMPROVES
- FATHERHOOD

LESSON #14

The Father Comes to the Children's Level to Better Understand

In my home, I like to spend a lot of my time in the living room. It's where we have the big TV and comfortable couch, it's carpeted, and everything is pretty much balanced in a cozy atmosphere. But for whatever reason, my two kids just love to crawl into the kitchen, and when they're in there, I can't see them, so I have to rely on my fatherly listening techniques to determine if I need to investigate further or if all is well. One dead giveaway that a master plot of mischief is developing between the two is when it's too quiet for any length of time. That's when I start barking questions as I try to get them to give up their coordinates without me having to give up my spot on the sofa to actually go see what they're doing.

When they don't give me a firm indication that they're clear of trouble, I sometimes go into the kitchen and sit on the floor with them to spend some time seeing life from their perspective. To my amazement, as much as I thought the kitchen floor was clean (and we do clean), the baseboards unspotted, and the appliances to be harmless, when I came down to do life at their level, it opens up a new world for me. In their world, I discover it's fascinating to put their fingers in the gap between the oven and the bottom broiler (when it's off of course), and ovens aren't the easiest appliance to keep clean. Also at this level, I can see they like to put their hands underneath the oven, and—goodness gracious—who knows what's all underneath there. They also like to try to reach as far as they can between the oven and the refrigerator to... Okay, without telling too much of my family's business, and to keep me off the couch tonight, my point is to say that when I come down to their level and see life as they see it, I better understand the complexity of their world. When I look at life from their angle, I can see all the hazards, all the things that look fun, all the temptations, and all the exciting things accessible to a person who lives in their world. As a benefit of me intimately experiencing their world in the way they like to experience it, I know now how to make things better for them overall. I know where to clean things up and how to help them do what they desire to do more safely and effectively.

This makes me think—among the millions of reasons why Our Father saw fit to send His Son down to live with us—about how His coming down to our level helps Him better understand us. Not only is He able to see and feel how it is for us to be tempted and sad, joyful and mad, but we are able to rest assured that He's been in the thick of things, just like us, and can relate to what's going on in our lives. Let's be grateful Our Father so loved us that He sent His Son to put on an earth suit of flesh and blood in order to experience life as we do, and in doing so, His compassion for us provides a clean path to the Father.

HEBREWS 2:16–18 (NLT)

> We also know that the Son did not come to help angels; he came to help the descendants of Abraham. Therefore, it was necessary for him to be made in every respect like us, his brothers and sisters, so that he could be our merciful and faithful High Priest before God. Then he could offer a sacrifice that would take away the sins of the people. Since he himself has gone through suffering and testing, he is able to help us when we are being tested.

THE FATHER COMES TO THE CHILDREN'S LEVEL TO BETTER UNDERSTAND

M	Q	Z	L	E	T	T	X	S	S	N	T	H	O	E
L	P	Y	E	K	W	U	O	K	Q	F	Y	T	C	M
H	P	C	V	C	J	N	I	O	E	L	N	B	U	Q
A	T	K	E	L	N	D	U	M	M	D	E	D	J	C
L	C	E	L	U	F	E	T	A	R	G	N	T	R	B
U	U	Z	M	X	F	R	I	E	B	E	W	Y	Y	Q
A	N	I	R	P	E	S	W	R	S	I	L	H	H	D
R	U	J	J	H	T	T	V	S	E	T	L	A	D	G
D	I	N	T	I	M	A	T	E	D	P	E	I	T	N
Z	C	A	S	V	O	N	T	G	I	E	X	D	T	E
V	F	S	C	Z	P	D	S	I	V	P	E	E	P	Y
Z	C	O	M	P	A	S	S	I	O	N	J	N	M	Q
Y	K	Y	S	Q	W	F	C	Z	R	N	N	I	X	L
P	V	L	Y	A	W	H	T	A	P	A	S	T	C	R
K	G	P	G	T	M	Q	J	D	N	D	E	V	F	X

SON
LEVEL
ABILITY
UNDERSTAND
RELATE
NEEDS
TEMPTATIONS
GRATEFUL
EXPERIENCE
COMPASSION
PROVIDES
PATHWAY
FATHER
INTIMATE
TESTED

LESSON #15

The Father's Thoughts Are Above Our Thoughts

Now that Jessica can crawl, she tends to follow me around the house, and no matter what I do, she's interested in the cause and effect of my actions. When I pick something up, she looks to see what it is, where it came from, and what I'm going to do with it. If I move ambitiously towards a room, she'll look at me and where I came from and follow me into the room to where I'm headed. She looks as if she wants to know what's going on, what am I doing, and what is happening in the process so she can get a better grasp of the situation.

Being the reasonable father I am, I don't mind talking to her and explaining my actions. It soon became clear to me that even when I tell her the "whats and whys" of my daily chores, she is not able to understand my explanations. Jessica is only six and a half months old and can't yet talk or understand English, so it doesn't matter if I include all the details, if I talk on a high level or in an abstract, profound way, she still won't have a clue about what I'm saying. In this case, it doesn't matter what words I choose for her because regardless of what I'm attempting to convey, she is not able to understand me at my level.

This revelation challenged me to consider the times when I want God to immediately tell me all the plans He has for my life—when I'm so bent on Him disclosing to me what's happening in this season and the details of what's coming up in the next. Exactly how will I accomplish this? Where will I fail? Then, I am confronted with the thought that even if He does reveal these spiritual truths to me, if they are beyond my scope of understanding, will they only confuse me more or, at best, create more questions and the need for more explanation? I'm aware that there are mysterious things that Our Father will reveal to us in His own sovereign timing, but I believe we need to exercise more patience and contentment in our zeal to control the unknown. Besides, truthfully speaking, if Our Father would have us know all the suffering we would have to endure before we choose to follow Him, would we say "yes" in advance?

ISAIAH 55:8–9 (NIV)

> "For My thoughts are not your thoughts, neither are your ways My ways," declares the LORD. "As the heavens are higher than the earth, so are My ways higher than your ways and My thoughts than your thoughts."

THE FATHER'S THOUGHTS ARE ABOVE OUR THOUGHTS

R	B	J	T	P	F	R	E	O	R	P	J	U	F	Z
C	Y	O	I	Q	U	E	S	T	I	O	N	S	G	F
W	E	B	B	X	T	V	Y	M	Z	D	O	V	C	Y
X	P	F	R	F	G	E	U	H	E	V	S	M	K	Z
B	O	E	N	O	L	L	R	R	E	T	O	O	C	L
E	C	N	A	V	D	A	S	R	H	K	V	Y	Z	U
L	S	D	X	L	V	T	E	G	J	I	S	I	J	N
L	O	U	A	X	A	I	U	Z	M	E	G	C	E	I
Y	Y	R	F	N	G	O	D	D	D	O	G	H	Q	U
K	K	E	D	N	H	N	I	M	E	N	R	I	E	Z
O	T	I	S	T	O	W	I	K	P	B	A	W	L	R
Y	N	L	Y	Y	N	C	Z	M	T	Z	W	X	J	Z
G	L	O	E	M	V	V	B	D	I	M	Y	L	W	X
F	K	B	E	S	T	F	S	K	C	T	E	H	U	Y
X	L	N	H	H	D	D	S	L	P	B	Z	X	U	B

- REVELATION
- ZEAL
- BEYOND
- SCOPE
- UNDERSTANDING
- CONFUSE
- QUESTIONS
- SOVEREIGN
- TIMING
- ENDURE
- YES
- ADVANCE
- THOUGHTS
- LORD
- HIGHER

LESSON #16

The Father Knows What It Takes to Get Your Attention

It was fairly early in the morning, and I was with my girlies, both dressed, fed, and ready to go out and do their thing in the world. Our routine for this morning: daycare for Jessica, therapy for Johannah, and then daycare for Johannah, but before this show could get on the road, I needed to get myself dressed. While they waited for me they were both sitting near the kitchen, and since Johannah has a real chill personality, I didn't have to worry about her getting into too much trouble while I was in my bedroom putting on clothes. Jessica, on the other hand, is very exploratory, which is a huge blessing, but because she is so curious, I need to have her follow me into the room so I can keep an eye on her.

To get Jessica to follow me into my bedroom, I had to first stand in the doorway and wave at her; then I called her by name until she gave me eye contact to let me know she heard me. So I said with my lightest, highest register, and friendliest voice, "Hi, Jessica, Hii, Jessie-ca...." This caused her to turn to me and give me her warmest three-toothed smile, and as soon as she smiled at me, I quickly dipped into my room. Being her father, I knew my sudden disappearance was going to pique her curiosity. She likes to investigate, so she's going to check to see where Daddy went. The entire purpose of me orchestrating this cat and mouse game is because I know my child and I want her to come to me; I want her to come find me, discover me, and to ultimately be with me.

In the same way, Our Father knew the exact way He had to call us unto Himself. What were your circumstances? Where were you located, and where did He have to take you? Are you the type to have to hit rock-bottom before you'll listen? Did He have to use your curiosity in a person, object, or substance? What compelled you to come to God? The Father always knows what it takes to get your attention, and He will use whatever is necessary to have you come running, scooting, or crawling closer to Him.

(P.S. As soon as she turned into my room, I scooped her up, hugged her, and kissed her all over her face—just like a father would.)

ACTS 17:27 (NLT)

" His purpose was for the nations to seek after God and perhaps feel their way toward Him and find Him—though He is not far from any one of us.

THE FATHER KNOWS WHAT IT TAKES TO GET YOUR ATTENTION

D	C	X	M	J	N	F	P	H	Y	L	N	U	O	F
T	O	L	R	M	J	S	P	T	Q	W	N	W	G	R
P	M	G	H	U	J	C	R	F	X	D	V	C	T	E
W	P	A	C	H	X	Q	U	X	E	D	Z	A	F	W
A	E	A	I	I	N	S	T	R	U	C	T	I	O	N
H	L	T	G	J	Y	S	S	G	I	U	U	B	D	X
L	L	T	A	K	E	T	K	F	Z	O	U	K	A	S
F	L	E	L	G	A	I	N	K	A	Z	S	O	U	D
O	E	N	G	N	I	N	N	U	R	T	C	I	I	V
M	M	T	D	E	A	T	O	X	O	G	H	S	T	H
Z	C	I	R	C	U	M	S	T	A	N	C	E	S	Y
R	N	O	B	O	G	D	I	E	E	O	A	E	R	O
G	B	N	E	Y	O	L	G	G	V	C	E	K	J	X
M	I	M	O	N	J	Y	N	E	V	N	R	B	F	W
M	H	M	S	N	V	B	R	N	R	O	I	F	A	H

- ATTENTION
- INSTRUCTION
- FATHER
- UNDERSTANDING
- CALL
- GAIN
- SON
- REACH
- SEEK
- COMPEL
- INVESTIGATE
- DISCOVER
- RUNNING
- CIRCUMSTANCES
- CURIOSITY

LESSON #17

The Father Opens and Closes Doors

Jessica is learning how to mimic our behavior. She's really catching on quickly, and that's a blessing. I've now begun to notice that after I've walked into a room and closed the door behind me because there are dangers in the room that I don't want to expose her to, she'll throw a temper tantrum and cry. The reason why I prohibit her from entering the room is because there could be things like a hot iron, sharp tools for a do-it-yourself project, or even wiry hangers hanging around, and none of these types of items make for a safe environment for a toddler. So I walk in, close the door, and she stands outside the door and cries.

Then there are other times when I'm not in the room but I'm nearby; she sees the door is open, so she accelerates into the room and closes the door on me. Once she gets into the room and closes the door, she soon realizes that although she has successfully shut me out, she does not know how to open the door for herself. Now she's stuck on the inside the room and can't get out but can hear me and the rest of the family on the outside together, so again she starts to cry for help. She cries because she is now faced with a closed door that she brought upon herself when trying to show me, her father, she can shut me out in the same manner she felt I've once closed the door on her. In this case, I know there is nothing in the room that can harm her, so I intentionally left the door open for her to freely come and go as she desired.

I've commonly heard people pray asking God to "close doors" of unknown catastrophes that He doesn't want us to go through and also for Him to "open doors" of opportunity that He would desire us to experience. For this to occur, we must learn to obey the still, small voice of Our Father's Spirit and not be so anxious to force ourselves into closed-door situations that leave us without the inner peace that comes from being with Him. That inner peace should also be evident in our conduct when He chooses to close a door we greatly desire to walk through because we are so used to having what we want.

REVELATION 3:7 (NIV)

 To the angel of the church in Philadelphia write: These are the words of Him who is Holy and True, who holds the key of David. What He opens no one can shut, and what He shuts no one can open.

THE FATHER OPENS AND CLOSES DOORS

Q	Z	Q	X	Y	F	O	L	Q	P	O	O	K	C	N
H	V	Q	B	N	N	J	P	Z	T	D	V	N	P	A
C	Z	G	Z	D	X	E	C	I	O	V	R	R	D	T
O	D	O	K	O	S	I	R	A	P	I	O	A	M	X
M	A	O	L	O	V	I	I	V	N	F	N	E	H	E
I	F	N	L	R	P	U	W	R	O	B	H	L	V	H
H	Z	C	Y	S	I	P	G	Z	J	P	E	R	G	K
R	M	C	I	W	F	R	O	E	O	B	E	Y	K	K
T	J	A	H	F	T	A	C	R	M	N	J	N	X	I
O	A	C	W	U	L	Y	T	W	T	U	H	S	F	M
D	Q	S	C	K	L	S	O	H	Z	U	J	R	Z	I
G	N	I	D	N	A	T	S	R	E	D	N	U	M	A
B	T	P	U	T	M	I	Q	Z	N	R	M	I	K	A
I	Q	Q	A	R	S	L	O	I	N	O	Q	H	T	J
C	F	C	F	R	Z	L	G	G	R	X	V	R	A	Y

- OPEN
- CLOSE
- DOOR
- SHUT
- FATHER
- UNDERSTANDING
- OBEY
- STILL
- SMALL
- VOICE
- PRAY
- OPPORTUNITY
- CATASTROPHE
- LEARN
- SPIRIT

LESSON #18

The Father Does What His Children Cannot Do

I was outside taking a stroll with my daughters; it was a good day, the 12th of October around 12:30 p.m., and I had both my girls. My wife was on a business trip to New York living her dream… God is good to our family. Being on "daddy day care" duty for the week helped me notice that sometimes when I correct Johannah's misbehavior, I'm starting to see Jessica, my youngest daughter, watch me and think she can do the same.

Ironically, I live my life before Jessica with the intent that sooner or later she will mimic my behavior. I pray that she mimics the best of how I live out my morals, communicate to others, manage myself, and show generosity. As any parent would, I pray she not only emulates these traits but ultimately will be greater than I am at doing them. But the problem with Jessica thinking she can correct her sister like I can is this: I'm not Johannah's sibling; I'm her father. It's my role to enforce the concepts of right and wrong that I have asked of Johannah while at the same time teaching them both boundaries about what is beneficial and permissible under my covering. When Jessica thinks she can correct her sister in the same way I do, then I'm going to promptly correct her through humility and deference. It is not her job to correct my children in the way I correct them because she is not the father. In her immaturity and inexperience, she may do more harm than good.

I believe Our Father desires the same trust from us to recognize He is better suited to discern the errors of people's hearts than we are. It is human nature that most of us carry biases that cause us to judge certain sins as being more acceptable than others. As a matter of course, we then assume harsher penalties for those behaviors we disagree with. Undoubtedly, God permits us to judge the spirit in which believers conduct themselves, but overall, it is God in us who gives us that discernment. As such, we should continually rely on Him to be our Judge and Master.

1 CORINTHIANS 4:4–5 (NLT)

> My conscience is clear, but that doesn't prove I'm right. It is the Lord himself who will examine me and decide. So don't make judgments about anyone ahead of time—before the Lord returns. For He will bring our darkest secrets to light and will reveal our private motives. Then God will give to each one whatever praise is due.

THE FATHER DOES WHAT HIS CHILDREN CANNOT DO

G	U	Y	X	V	X	P	T	H	X	G	E	N	B	E
U	M	M	F	A	B	L	O	S	H	L	U	O	E	B
V	V	P	A	U	S	Z	A	U	U	M	W	I	E	C
E	A	T	F	V	E	X	G	I	Q	R	K	T	T	C
M	A	F	P	L	S	Q	S	T	Z	R	T	I	O	F
V	I	C	T	F	E	I	L	E	B	E	G	N	P	S
V	I	O	I	R	Y	V	R	D	R	L	S	G	K	P
M	B	L	A	B	I	L	I	T	Y	Y	I	F	O	Q
G	J	K	X	Q	W	S	N	F	S	A	S	C	M	W
Z	O	H	A	C	C	E	P	T	A	N	C	E	O	M
Y	M	K	X	E	M	L	E	A	A	C	N	R	D	P
U	I	D	R	G	I	N	E	X	C	E	E	D	S	C
Z	K	N	D	W	C	J	T	S	F	A	N	T	I	R
D	Q	U	E	Y	K	H	J	R	D	Y	P	R	W	Y
Q	J	E	G	N	G	S	U	Y	X	K	K	K	F	F

- ABILITY
- EXCEEDS
- DESIRES
- BELIEF
- TRUST
- RECOGNITION
- READY
- ACCEPTANCE
- BETTER
- SUITED
- DISCERN
- JUDGMENT
- WISDOM
- CONSISTENCY
- RELIANCE

LESSON #19

The Father's Gifts Come With Responsibility

Jessica is really developing quickly these days and I'm noticing there are a lot of things that she's catching on to. In particular one thing that comes to mind is how well she is crawling and how much faster and quicker she can get around the house. She knows the different rooms in the house and can easily flow from the living room to the bedrooms to the kitchen. This is really exceptional given she's only 6 1/2 months now, matter of fact she will be dedicated back to the Lord this coming Sunday, so these are quite advanced skills to an onlooking father.

In my delight I've also noticed that the higher she goes in her developmental process there are more everyday dangers accessible to her. When she crawls into the kitchen because she's mobile now, it's dangerous there. When she pulls up on the TV stand it's dangerous there, and the couch sometimes have objects on it that can present a concern too. So as a father I've realized there are many different things she can grab ahold of that may hurt her, and there are a variety of places she can go that can bring her harm. However, her accessibility to these dangers are in direct response to her proper growth and advancement in life.

This reminds me of our relationship with Our Father. Our blessings are synonymous with more responsibility. The more we mature and grow in life the more we must become even wiser, more discerning, and more aware of the world around us. He does not desire for us to shrink in the face of challenge or adversity but to grow in our confidence and strength in the ability He has given us to overcome. I pray boldness in your growth, determination in your journey, faith in yourself and in the Father as you triumph in your spiritual and practical development.

ISAIAH 41:9B-10

" For I have chosen you and will not throw you away. Don't be afraid, for I am with you. Don't be discouraged, for I am your God. I will strengthen you and help you. I will hold you up with My victorious right hand."

THE FATHER'S GIFTS COME WITH RESPONSIBILITY

Y	B	M	E	R	A	O	H	S	J	E	O	B	F	Y
Q	D	P	B	F	T	V	T	Y	X	L	F	N	T	V
X	F	A	L	M	W	F	B	L	E	S	S	I	N	G
N	V	Q	N	C	I	M	I	M	V	N	L	B	E	Q
O	Q	Y	P	G	S	F	O	F	A	I	R	Y	M	J
B	R	C	M	K	E	C	X	A	B	T	T	U	P	J
C	X	R	I	O	R	R	S	I	O	I	U	D	O	U
H	T	G	N	E	R	T	S	U	L	F	G	R	L	J
U	C	P	V	C	O	N	F	I	D	E	N	C	E	L
P	Z	O	L	S	O	R	B	G	N	J	Z	Z	V	K
Y	L	I	I	P	P	A	N	D	E	B	C	T	E	H
E	C	C	S	H	R	I	N	K	S	O	W	X	D	K
U	V	E	N	I	T	Z	E	E	S	B	T	S	E	M
K	R	L	F	D	Q	H	F	M	N	C	Q	C	R	E
G	W	N	E	A	Q	C	B	T	R	V	P	Z	S	U

- ABILITY
- BLESSING
- BOLDNESS
- CONFIDENCE
- DANGERS
- DEVELOPMENT
- GIFTS
- JOURNEY
- LIFE
- MATURE
- OVERCOME
- RESPONSIBILITY
- SHRINK
- STRENGTH
- WISER

LESSON #20

What Are You Keeping From the Father?

These days when Jessica has something that she knows either I or my wife wants, like our cell phones or keys, she can recognize she has stumbled upon something good and will posture herself to be able to keep whatever she has found. It's both cute and trivial to see her sneaky grin smile at me, on the verge of giggling, casually showing me that she knows she has a big ticket item in her hands. I think in her child mind, she thinks because she's found it, she now has rights to it and should be able to keep it and play with it as she does with her other toys.

This is where it gets interesting. When I see what she has, I'll call her—"Jessica!"—and as soon as she hears her name, she'll take off running because she doesn't want me to take her new find from her. Now, from my fatherly perspective, I see she has something that is really mine, but she does not want me to take it from her, so she makes me chase her down in order to get it from her. She is only an infant, so most of the time her stride doesn't get her out of the room, but I can see she's trying her best to keep the item away from me. Then when I finally take back what is legitimately mine, she will cry and fuss and look at me like I'm taking away something that belongs to her and brings her joy—the reasons why she was keeping it from me in the first place.

How often do we keep things, situations, and people away from our heavenly Father that we know He wants from us? How long have you been running from His process of removing those things that He hasn't yet intended for you? Have you gotten to a point where you think you are entitled to the objects you've attained? More importantly, will you accuse God of being malicious if He removes the collection of stuff that wasn't in His plans for you in the first place? It's time we stop running from Him and hand it all over to the Father, trusting He will only remove those things He knows are not for us.

PSALM 139:23–24 (NLT)

 Search me, O God, and know my heart; test me and know my anxious thoughts. Point out anything in me that offends You, and lead me along the path of everlasting life.

WHAT ARE YOU KEEPING FROM THE FATHER?

S	I	T	U	A	T	I	O	N	S	I	Z	X	M	F
N	Y	E	I	U	D	D	C	R	G	W	E	P	J	J
E	G	V	Q	M	F	A	S	N	N	B	K	F	L	H
O	I	O	R	G	B	E	G	P	I	H	R	F	X	L
N	R	M	W	H	D	U	D	O	H	H	E	C	P	C
Y	W	E	C	J	B	C	S	F	T	I	Y	V	K	R
Y	B	R	H	H	H	D	H	K	R	D	G	K	H	A
T	S	U	R	T	L	E	L	P	O	E	P	K	Z	K
E	F	N	H	V	A	M	J	B	B	A	P	I	W	G
L	V	N	M	V	O	F	S	L	W	U	D	S	E	N
F	U	I	E	R	U	T	A	M	A	V	R	J	S	V
K	I	N	G	D	O	M	U	X	W	H	X	P	A	N
L	L	G	N	P	E	Z	W	B	Z	U	A	C	H	R
Y	Z	I	M	Q	W	W	P	Q	I	I	X	T	Z	L
S	E	G	N	G	K	G	Q	R	Z	F	S	O	H	Z

- HIDE
- THINGS
- SITUATIONS
- PEOPLE
- STOP
- RUNNING
- BLAME
- SUBMIT
- GIVE
- TRUST
- HEAVENLY
- FATHER
- MATURE
- KINGDOM
- REMOVE

LESSON #21

There Is No Hiding From the Father

My daughter Johannah reminds me so much of "us" and how we behave as Christians. For example, whenever she wants to do something that she knows she isn't supposed to do, especially if she knows it's something that I don't like (such as sucking her thumb), she will crawl somewhere out of my line of sight to do it.

So if I'm sitting on the couch in the living room and I see her sucking her thumb, I'll say in my authoritative voice, "Johannah!" and she'll immediately snatch her thumb out of her mouth and move about on the floor as if she was doing something completely unrelated. Then when she thinks I'm no longer focused on her and she wants to resume doing what she knows she isn't permitted to do, she'll crawl to the back side of a large exercise ball we have in our living room so I can't see her nor is she able to see me. Every now and again she will lean to the side of the ball and look back towards me to make sure that I'm still where I was when she last saw me and then lean back directly behind the ball so she's out of view and able to continue to suck her thumb.

It is only when I lean to the side to see where she's moved to that she will then recognize that I can see her and instantly snatch her thumb out of her mouth and pretend to be interested in a toy or book that's nearby. As her father, it is somewhat puzzling, yet entertaining, how she thinks she can outmaneuver me in our small living room by using a ball that I can easily kick, remove, or destroy as I see fit. Further to this point, little does she know that behind her is a sliding glass door that casts her reflection, so I technically don't have to move the ball to know exactly what she's doing. But for some odd reason she finds security in thinking she can hide from me in order to disobey my requests.

I wonder if this is similar to how we are seen by Our Father when we try to hide our wrongdoings, insecurities, and problems from Him, thinking we can handle it on our own. It is our natural response to act like we know better than He does when it comes to doing what we want in life, particularly when we have opposing views and our view seems more logical, convenient, or beneficial to us. Since Our Father is always everywhere at once, I pray we lay down our pride and confess our weaknesses to Him. This way, instead of cloaking them in secrecy, we allow Him to intervene and be God of our daily struggles. He always knows where we are and what we're doing, whether it's good or bad. The world is His creation in the first place. Let's learn to live in plain sight of His correction, forgiveness, and love.

PSALM 139:7–10 (NLT)

" I can never escape from your Spirit! I can never get away from your presence! If I go up to heaven, You are there; if I go down to the grave, You are there. If I ride the wings of the morning, if I dwell by the farthest oceans, even there Your hand will guide me, and Your strength will support me.

THERE IS NO HIDING FROM THE FATHER

Y	R	G	S	O	G	J	P	O	K	T	I	E	X	J
V	O	E	C	H	R	T	N	T	N	N	L	H	P	R
M	T	N	O	H	E	W	B	Y	S	O	O	R	I	P
O	A	E	N	S	S	E	N	E	V	I	G	R	O	F
P	E	V	F	Y	T	T	C	E	Q	T	Q	K	R	F
B	R	R	E	P	O	U	T	I	V	C	I	T	V	C
O	C	E	S	T	R	U	G	G	L	E	S	I	U	L
E	B	T	S	I	E	F	B	B	Y	R	M	O	F	G
W	D	N	T	E	R	E	H	W	Y	R	E	V	E	R
K	E	I	I	V	N	S	W	X	X	O	L	E	M	O
T	E	Q	R	M	Q	C	P	Z	X	C	B	Z	W	Q
S	Y	F	I	P	J	A	E	O	X	L	O	T	O	R
Y	V	S	P	L	L	E	L	A	K	E	R	M	K	C
T	B	Y	S	R	S	E	G	G	O	X	P	N	F	I
M	B	A	A	T	W	D	E	U	I	C	U	U	X	W

- ESCAPE
- STRUGGLES
- CORRECTION
- FORGIVENESS
- LOVE
- SPIRIT
- PRESENCE
- EVERYWHERE
- INSECURITIES
- PROBLEMS
- CREATOR
- CONFESS
- PRIDE
- INTERVENE
- RESTORE

LESSON #22

The Father Has Us in Places to Influence Others

It's amazing the things kids find around the house that you had no idea existed. Quite often these days when Johannah and Jessica are roaming around the house, they'll pick up random items like old food, forgotten electronic gadgets, and bits and pieces of furniture projects that have been left everywhere. Sometimes I see them unearth old pieces of paper from under the couch or from behind the TV stand, and it makes me think about how, although I'm the father in this house and I'm technically able to see everything they see, in a way I still rely on their viewpoint to help me understand what's all going on under my own roof.

It's through them and their perspective, their purview, and their "world" that they contribute a level of attention and detail helpful for me to better understand our surroundings. They're able to close in on places in our home that I am responsible for in general but that only they relate to daily and touch specifically. I realize I need them to see those things, or I may miss them all together. From my vantage point, I'm not always aware of the nuts and bolts of a matter, so having a child tuned into that world helps me understand it better.

I believe this is the same reason why God has put us in places and in circles that our pastors and leaders are not in or welcomed at. He's uniquely placed us in spaces where other ministers are not accustomed to being and in locations where people may not even want to hear about God to begin with. It's in these pockets of influential places where people would rather hear about you and, in turn, how your life experiences reflect Him.

Our Father knows we have a level of engagement and a level of attention for details in the lives of the people we care about. It's in these connections that we can share a perspective of Our Father's love that others may not feel they can relate to God "The Father" on because their issues are too trivial and He has bigger matters to attend to. To them, Our Father can be seen as a "supervisor in the sky," so when He seeks to have an intimate relationship with them, it falls on deaf ears and hardened hearts.

But since we have been placed in a specific sphere of influence, there are certain trusts people may not easily surrender to Our Father, but they are willing to trust God in us with the details of their soul. It then becomes our duty to be extensions of Our Father's hands and provide Him with the prayer requests of our peers. Through relationship, we can help them connect with God on a level they understand by watching our prayer life, discipling, and Godly living. This way He can use us to minister from our perspective, from our worldview, and through our common life experiences. The best part of this is that we're equipped to do this just where we are, just how we're dressed, in order to touch people just like us.

MATTHEW 5:14–16 (NLT)

You are the light of the world—like a city on a hilltop that cannot be hidden. No one lights a lamp and then puts it under a basket. Instead, a lamp is placed on a stand, where it gives light to everyone in the house. In the same way, let your good deeds shine out for all to see, so that everyone will praise your heavenly Father.

THE FATHER HAS US IN PLACES TO INFLUENCE OTHERS

Y	F	O	A	Z	E	W	N	G	D	Q	P	M	W	B
T	E	E	C	N	E	U	L	F	N	I	S	P	Q	X
T	P	J	E	C	B	F	X	S	H	A	R	I	N	G
C	O	W	O	R	K	E	R	S	N	M	Y	P	P	D
M	H	I	Q	V	M	I	N	I	S	T	R	Y	R	P
L	A	S	L	R	I	O	J	S	E	N	C	H	Z	O
S	R	E	V	E	I	L	E	B	G	N	I	V	I	L
K	E	L	G	T	G	L	R	G	E	T	D	O	C	I
I	P	Y	A	V	P	T	U	O	L	L	T	S	J	Q
R	J	L	R	M	T	S	T	O	J	R	Y	G	S	Y
H	E	G	A	G	N	E	U	J	U	I	M	S	E	Y
R	Z	X	Q	C	O	P	F	S	S	L	I	U	Z	O
N	E	E	D	H	E	X	T	E	Q	A	G	O	K	X
U	K	R	V	B	X	S	N	N	N	H	O	F	G	S
N	R	W	B	H	N	K	R	V	R	Q	X	U	N	P

- WISELY
- PLACES
- TRUSTS
- MINISTRY
- SHARING
- INFLUENCE
- ENGAGE
- BELIEVERS
- FRIENDS
- COWORKERS
- LIVING
- EXAMPLES
- RELATIONSHIP
- HOPE
- FUTURE

LESSON #23

The Great and Terrible Father

I've learned that I have to be very careful with the volume and tone of my voice when it comes to communicating with my children. Sometimes when my girls are both playing in the living room and one of them does something inappropriate, I'll quickly shout "STOP!" and in that one word, I can feel the atmosphere vibrate and the room become tense. Usually, before I express my objection, the girls are light-heartedly playing or exploring around the house. So when my voice catches them off guard, both jump and look at me to see what my concern is and, more importantly, who I am concerned with.

The one who knows she's been caught doing something I don't approve of can immediately see it in my eyes and feel it through my voice that's she's on the wrong side of my goodwill. When this happens, she immediately switches her behavior to an activity that won't require further discipline. Conversely, after looking at me, my other child, who knows the corrective command did not concern her and who knows she is not in trouble for doing anything wrong, will simply turn back around and continue playing with her toy as if to say, "That has nothing to do with me."

This makes me think about the great day when Our Father will decide to bring all His children back unto Himself. For those that have been living in disobedience, when they hear His voice, it will be a dreadful sound, and they will tremble in fear of His eternal punishment. But for those that have chosen to live according to His will and have accepted Him as Father, they will hear His great voice and rejoice that He has returned to make all things new, just like He said He would.

JOEL 2:11 (NIV)

 The LORD thunders at the head of His army; His forces are beyond number, and mighty is the army that obeys His command. The day of the LORD is great; it is dreadful. Who can endure it?

THE GREAT AND TERRIBLE FATHER

M	Y	M	B	Y	V	D	I	P	P	R	D	W	X	R
V	U	Z	T	D	H	E	L	L	V	E	F	S	E	E
Y	Q	I	B	S	E	S	J	K	M	C	M	J	R	C
C	E	Q	R	L	A	U	W	I	E	H	O	G	Z	W
I	C	Z	E	L	V	G	P	P	U	I	M	L	O	T
N	O	I	T	C	E	R	R	O	C	S	J	S	G	M
V	M	P	U	C	N	E	R	E	H	J	X	V	W	Z
U	M	Y	R	I	G	A	A	F	O	B	E	Y	P	J
J	A	P	N	S	Q	T	T	B	I	E	C	G	Z	P
S	N	D	E	N	Q	A	H	P	C	D	Y	U	B	V
Y	D	H	D	Q	A	P	S	G	E	V	N	F	O	L
L	C	M	X	P	N	C	S	K	O	C	U	I	O	N
T	Z	V	C	T	S	J	M	C	R	Y	C	R	W	L
N	M	B	G	J	Q	V	O	Q	E	E	F	A	M	D
J	Y	S	H	J	R	M	M	S	H	C	N	M	Q	C

- VOICE
- COMMAND
- CORRECTION
- ACCEPTANCE
- HEAVEN
- RETURNED
- HIS
- GREAT
- VOICE
- REJOICE
- RETURN
- OBEY
- CHOICE
- HEAVEN
- HELL

LESSON #24

In a World Of Noise, the Father Knows His Children's Cries

This past Sunday was what we as a church family call "Consecration Sunday." It's the culmination of 21 days of prayer and fasting that starts at the beginning of the year and is deemed a "first fruits" offering to the Lord. We intentionally practice this first thing in a new year because we are fasting and praying to seek His presence first in all areas of our lives. So on Consecration Sunday, our order of service is a little different than our typical Sunday services. Specifically, we do something called "high church." That's when we dress up in our official uniforms based on the offices we serve in the church and have formal processionals and recessionals to start and end the service. On this day, you'll see pastors, ministers, mothers, deacons, deaconesses, and ushers dressed quite fancifully with the Bishop in his traditional priest regalia to boot.

So there I was, a pastor in my uniform, in the front row of the church, and since I had to come early, I didn't exactly know where my family ended up sitting within the congregation. Also, to add to the festiveness, my wife's parents were in town to celebrate my youngest daughter Jessica's first birthday, which was the previous Friday.

As I was sitting there, I could hear my daughter Johannah blurt out a loud yell. In a crowd of thousands (our church can serve around 2,500 people at a time, and it was full this day, so much so that there were people in an overflow area), I could hear my daughter's cry, and by the sound of it, I could determine what she wanted. Her cry was one that said, "I want attention, I'm bored, and if you have something to feed me, I'll take it, but I'm really just restless and want to play, but you have me here in this place where no one is playing. Everyone is just sitting down and listening to a loud voice, so I'm going to make some noise and have some fun and do something different to stimulate myself." Yes, I can hear all that in a cry.

Again, I heard this through the background noises in a crowd of thousands, but I knew there was nothing I could do about it at the moment because I was in the front row of a very special ceremonial day. More importantly, I also knew there was nothing that I *had to do* about it because I know that type of cry and I knew whom she had with her. She had her mother and her grandparents, so I knew she was well taken care of for any scenario that would cause that sort of cry.

Empowered with this intimate awareness that comes with being her father, I shifted my attitude about her holler, and it actually made me begin to smile. I smiled because knowing her voice regardless of our proximity to each other lets me know that I'm closely connected to her. I'm connected because I've been with her through numerous occasions, in a variety of life situations, and have heard that cry before. She's been in my arms, by my side, in my presence, and one on one, and she's made that cry and other cries that I'm also uniquely attentive to. Because of this relationship, when I heard my child's voice, I just sat there and smiled, thinking, *That's my baby girl.*

This is the same way it is with us and our heavenly Father. He hears our cry in a world of billions and billions. He knows our cry and our specific situation, and He knows just where we are and who is with us while we're going through life's challenges. Our Father knows what we can handle. He's a loving Father who cares for us. He's purposefully placed different resources and people in our lives to guarantee us that we can make it through this too. When we feel unheard, we can rest assured that He's paying close attention. He may not change everything in that moment to cater to us as we may expect, but please know He's listening, He's observing, He's smiling, and He's ALWAYS loving you.

PSALM 116:1–2 (NIV)

"I love the LORD, for He heard my voice; He heard my cry for mercy. Because He turned his ear to me, I will call on Him as long as I live.

IN A WORLD OF NOISE, THE FATHER KNOWS HIS CHILDREN'S CRIES

L	V	M	D	A	S	R	I	S	H	I	S	O	P	C
V	I	I	R	E	P	B	H	P	M	O	C	U	H	N
Z	W	S	R	N	R	E	V	E	N	I	F	I	S	E
R	E	H	T	A	F	O	V	O	S	P	L	C	V	F
V	H	Z	W	E	G	V	N	P	S	D	X	I	W	U
G	G	E	O	K	N	O	D	L	R	O	W	K	N	R
I	N	L	R	I	I	I	Q	E	H	E	U	H	F	G
V	I	V	F	S	V	L	N	J	Q	A	X	V	H	G
R	V	H	E	A	R	I	N	G	G	Y	S	H	S	U
N	O	I	T	N	E	T	T	A	X	X	S	L	J	C
B	L	O	C	K	S	R	H	L	E	E	U	L	T	A
F	L	C	E	E	B	G	W	R	I	O	T	P	Z	R
S	E	C	R	U	O	S	E	R	P	U	L	I	Y	H
U	A	T	K	C	N	H	C	S	Q	R	T	X	L	F
H	Y	U	I	C	J	X	W	B	C	G	I	F	E	T

- WORLD
- NOISE
- NEVER
- BLOCKS
- FATHER
- HEARING
- CRIES
- CHILDREN
- LISTENING
- OBSERVING
- SMILING
- LOVING
- ATTENTION
- PEOPLE
- RESOURCES

LESSON #25

In the Father's Wisdom, He Gives His Children Everything in Due Time

I continue to notice that my children like doing things they see me doing, and that's a beautiful part of parenting and a sign of their progress. But I'm also starting to realize that while it's ideal for them to model my behavior, there are some things that I do—and that they want to do—that can be bad for them without proper training and care.

For instance, when ironing my clothes, I use an iron with a retractable cord that makes a real fun sound when it's extended and when it retracts. This really entertains the kids, but as adults, we know irons are hot and heavy and could fall, causing considerable damage if mishandled by the cord. This is why when I'm ironing, the ironing area becomes a strict no kids zone. Matter of fact, we put up barriers so they can't come around, but if somehow they get through the barrier, then they are reminded this area is "**not** for Jessica" or "**not** for Johannah."

Gradually, it began to sink into my mind that it will not always be this way for them. Eventually they will be able to use the iron and other potentially hazardous appliances with no problem. Even now there have been things in their younger lives, like certain toys or eating utensils, that were restricted until they matured, and now that they've grown, some of those things are now acceptable for them to use. Actually, everything in my house is for them once they reach a certain level of maturity. However, until they can handle these more threatening items with proper care, understanding, and responsibility, then it's best they do not have access to them at all.

In much the same way, Our Father has given us everything on earth to rule and have dominion over. But not everything on earth is right for us to have right now. As we mature in the Spirit through self-control, understanding, and respect for the world around us, then He will make accessible to us more of the provisions He has already destined for us. This includes desired relationships, promotions, business deals, and ministry opportunities, among other things.

Although we may struggle with His timing due to our lack of patience, if He gives us what we want too early, we can hurt ourselves even with His gifts. It is Our Father's wisdom and love that prompts Him to pay close attention to the maturity of His children. It is through Our Father's foresight that He sees what to give us now to help us blossom and flourish. Our Father uses discernment to know what He needs to hold back from us, although we may cry and complain when He doesn't give us what we want to enjoy in life.

Regardless, Our Father provides what we need to live our best lives now. But as we mature and demonstrate the ability to manage more, He will even trust us with the things He wisely held back from us to protect us, and through them we will bring Him glory.

PSALM 84:11–12 (NLT)

> For the LORD God is our sun and our shield. He gives us grace and glory. The LORD will withhold no good thing from those who do what is right. O LORD of Heaven's Armies, what joy for those who trust in you.

IN THE FATHER'S WISDOM, HE GIVES HIS CHILDREN EVERYTHING IN DUE TIME

X	Y	L	N	G	Z	E	P	I	B	H	B	O	H	B
R	O	A	J	T	C	R	C	U	V	G	I	G	K	X
E	O	I	B	I	A	C	N	N	E	G	V	Q	X	L
H	O	U	E	C	N	E	I	T	A	P	R	V	N	Z
T	C	E	T	O	R	P	D	J	O	D	T	X	D	I
A	A	I	I	D	W	R	L	P	F	G	I	T	X	M
F	C	G	L	O	L	P	R	A	C	T	R	U	S	T
E	Z	I	L	A	E	R	V	F	K	K	D	O	G	Q
X	H	L	H	O	N	O	R	X	Y	J	J	V	W	L
C	O	I	H	V	R	V	K	M	U	G	F	T	M	I
F	T	C	B	W	P	I	O	O	X	D	X	Q	W	Q
D	Q	T	N	D	C	D	F	O	C	X	N	E	U	H
L	O	H	E	U	E	E	R	Y	X	R	E	A	J	Z
W	N	J	S	L	S	F	B	P	J	P	G	F	W	A
E	D	M	M	F	D	N	M	D	X	U	G	N	V	Y

- PRACTICE
- REALIZE
- FOLLOW
- PATIENCE
- TRUST
- FAVOR
- HONOR
- GLORIFY
- FATHER
- MODEL
- PROTECT
- CHILDREN
- PROVIDE
- GUIDANCE
- GROW

LESSON #26

Sometimes the Father Doesn't Make "IT" Easy so You Won't Take "IT" for Granted

At night I place my mobile phone next to me on my bed frame, and there is a small gap between my bed frame and the mattress. Now, lucky me, Jessica typically wakes me up in the morning, and when she does, she'll sometimes see my phone and immediately get distracted and go to play with it. Nine times out of ten, when she goes for the phone, she doesn't fully grab it but rather she accidentally pushes it into the gap between my bed frame and the mattress. When she does this, I have to immediately reach in between and get it out or else I'll forget it and go to work without my phone. Then it will instantly become *"one of those days."*

So this Christmas Jessica received a toy phone of her own. Her phone has Elmo, Sesame Street, ABCs, 123s, and other children songs on it. This morning as she came to wake me up, I could see her creep through the door, and this time she had her phone with her. She then proceeded to put her phone in the same gap that she typically knocks mine into. I thought this was humorously ironic for her to somehow think that this space was an appropriate "phone gap" to place phones into. My children continually crack me up.

But here's the problem—when Jessica puts her phone in the gap, she can't get it out. I've gotten it out for her once or twice, but when I do, she immediately puts it back in. Again I'd get it out, and again she'd put it back in. So I decided I would no longer get her phone out of the gap for her. In doing so, I see her start to make many attempts to get her phone out of the phone gap herself. I can see her begin to struggle, whine, and get frustrated, but once she finally gets it out, guess what happens? She doesn't put it back in.

She doesn't want a repeat of the angst or frustration of taking something out of an undesirable place, even though all along I have been trying to keep it out of that same place for her countless times. It turns out that if I continue to provide an easy solution for her without her having to contribute to that solution, then she considers it fun and without consequence. But when I stop making it easy for her and she toils with the process of removing something undesirable for herself, under my supervision, then she learns for herself how it's not a good idea to get in that situation in the first place.

I believe our Father guides us in a similar way. He desires that we mature and be made wiser and more responsible by participating in the process of Him growing us. We should embrace Our Father's prevention, protection, wisdom, and deliverance so we can minimize the pitfalls of life and maximize the joy and favor of His intervention.

1 PETER 1:6–7 (NIV)

> In all this you greatly rejoice, though now for a little while you may have had to suffer grief in all kinds of trials. These have come so that the proven genuineness of your faith—of greater worth than gold, which perishes even though refined by fire—may result in praise, glory and honor when Jesus Christ is revealed.

SOMETIMES THE FATHER DOESN'T MAKE "IT" EASY SO YOU WON'T TAKE "IT" FOR GRANTED

O	A	E	W	V	R	S	T	R	E	T	C	H	G	X
G	Y	A	P	I	B	E	L	L	F	O	T	P	U	M
M	R	A	V	R	S	Z	R	L	N	V	B	Z	O	W
C	D	O	O	H	R	E	H	T	A	F	M	O	T	U
C	O	A	W	H	U	Z	R	H	V	F	A	N	F	K
L	B	L	E	S	S	I	N	G	S	E	T	O	H	D
C	K	S	E	E	B	M	O	E	Z	E	U	I	E	C
G	N	V	O	U	X	I	G	I	M	I	R	T	P	R
U	U	E	T	R	U	N	M	F	B	Z	I	U	E	W
Q	Z	I	B	O	R	I	Q	W	P	L	T	L	H	J
E	O	R	D	V	X	M	Y	T	G	B	Y	O	J	G
N	S	B	X	A	A	H	T	U	Q	B	X	S	E	J
Q	A	P	M	F	N	I	J	J	B	I	F	K	O	I
A	W	W	T	Z	N	C	Q	L	G	C	U	L	B	K
Z	O	S	S	P	Q	F	E	I	P	K	X	P	B	M

- STRETCH
- GROW
- RELY
- GUIDANCE
- WISER
- BLESSINGS
- MINIMIZE
- PITFALLS
- MAXIMIZE
- JOY
- FAVOR
- MATURITY
- FATHERHOOD
- SOLUTION
- CONTRIBUTION

LESSON #27

What the Father Has Prepared for You Is Only for You

My youngest girl, Jessica, is able to drink from a sippy cup. If you know anything about the design of sippy cups, you know they're cleverly made in such a way that they can tip over and not spill their contents. The reason they're able to retain liquids like water, juice, and milk is because they require suction in order to allow the fluid in the cup to be released. Since Jessica likes to move about the house drinking her milk, it's best she uses her sippy cup to keep from making a mess all over the place. Although Jessica knows how to drink from a sippy cup, Johannah doesn't. We desire Johannah to learn how to use one very soon, but for now, she drinks out of a bottle.

We also think Johannah is lactose intolerant and have not been giving her milk for some time now even though she really likes to drink it. With this in mind, I gave Jessica some milk in her sippy cup and gave Johannah a bottle of apple juice and water (2 oz. apple juice, 6 oz. water). Johannah quickly finished her apple juice water, but Jessica still had milk left in her sippy cup, so Johannah tried to take the remaining portion of Jessica's milk. When Jessica saw Johannah grab her sippy cup, she looked at me and complained as if to say, "Dad, you see Johannah's trying to take my milk, right?" Now, Jessica isn't powerful enough to take the cup back from Johannah; if Johannah wants something, she's strong enough to take it and keep it. This threw Jessica into a craze as she pointed at her sister and looked at me. I calmly looked over and saw that the milk was in the sippy cup.

Then it dawned on me that even though Johannah had what belonged to Jessica, Johannah couldn't benefit from what belonged to her sister. This is because what I gave to Jessica was for Jessica, and what I gave to Johannah was for Johannah. Even though Johannah has more muscle and brute strength to take it away from Jessica, as their father, I know that what I intended for Jessica can only be used by Jessica. No matter how overpowering she may seem, Johannah cannot gain from what was not intended for her.

This reminds me of how Our Father has specifically equipped us for our life's journey. He has given us different gifts, abilities, talents, favor, relationships, and positions designed and appointed just for us. And although there may be other people that are more qualified, stronger, smarter, or connected, they cannot prosper from the things Our Father has intended for us. Take time today to thank God for His divine will, His providence, His sovereignty, and His favor.

1 CORINTHIANS 2:9B (NLT)

"No eye has seen, no ear has heard, and no mind has imagined what God has prepared for those who love Him.

WHAT THE FATHER HAS PREPARED FOR YOU IS ONLY FOR YOU

G	K	A	T	W	P	Q	S	M	S	D	G	E	V	M
W	Z	Q	T	S	H	K	U	N	R	N	V	Z	P	J
L	N	W	Y	P	O	S	I	T	I	O	N	S	N	U
U	P	X	P	B	C	V	U	R	B	E	L	L	B	I
U	D	O	R	L	P	S	E	I	T	I	L	I	B	A
L	M	E	E	O	O	W	Z	R	G	E	B	J	D	D
O	Y	J	P	R	O	V	I	D	E	N	C	E	E	E
R	H	N	A	P	P	U	S	W	B	I	O	N	D	Z
E	T	U	R	B	I	R	I	T	H	V	G	L	N	B
P	C	E	E	M	L	U	W	R	B	I	Z	N	E	T
S	V	R	D	M	U	H	Q	H	S	D	C	N	T	B
O	P	H	S	O	M	X	D	E	F	B	E	V	N	Y
R	G	A	E	Y	W	I	D	N	R	F	I	C	I	Q
P	W	U	M	I	U	L	Q	Z	I	R	F	W	N	M
V	J	I	Q	C	R	L	L	T	K	Q	E	N	K	J

- PREPARED
- BELONG
- BENEFIT
- MUSCLE
- BRUTE
- OVERPOWERING
- INTENDED
- EQUIPPED
- PROVIDENCE
- SOVEREIGNTY
- PROSPER
- DESIGNED
- POSITIONS
- ABILITIES
- DIVINE

LESSON #28

Father, Keep Your Hand On Me

In my home I'm in charge of the morning time routine, it's when I change Jessica's and Johannah's diapers and get them dressed and prepared for the day. Typically I change them on our changing table which is about three and a half feet tall and around four feet wide. It just so happened that during this morning's prep time Jessica decided to kick a dirty diaper off the changing table (thankfully I had already tied it up) so I bent down to pick it up before my other child got a hold of it. As I reached down with my left hand to pick up the dirty diaper, I was careful to feel around for Jessica with my right hand on the top of the table because there is a rule that says anytime you have a child on a raised surface you must keep at least one hand on them. So now as I'm leaning down picking up the dirty diaper, my head and eyes are downward but my other hand is on top of the table trying to locate her. Suddenly I feel her hand grab my hand and put it on her chest. Ahh, there she is.

In that moment she completely inspired me. Immediately a prayer to Our Father entered my heart. "Hey Lord, You have me on this raised surface of life and I know You are doing a lot of things around me, changing a lot of things in me, and handling my mess in the process. So if You're reaching around in my direction to ensure I am in the right place where You are preparing me for greatness, while providing the safety of Your touch when I can't see You, then I'm going to do all I can to help You find me because I want Your hand on me. I need Your hand on my life. Your hand keeps me safe, it keeps me grounded, keeps me secure and keeps me warm. Your hand lets me know I am loved... Father, please, keep Your hand on me."

ISAIAH 41:9-10

" I have called you back from the ends of the earth, saying, 'You are My servant.' For I have chosen you and will not throw you away. Don't be afraid, for I am with you. Don't be discouraged, for I am your God. I will strengthen you and help you. I will hold you up with My victorious right hand."

FATHER, KEEP YOUR HAND ON ME

A	A	V	M	W	M	N	I	D	W	Z	Y	Q	K	Q
N	L	P	H	Y	H	Y	X	N	H	W	V	R	E	Y
N	Y	O	P	M	S	L	P	S	S	I	X	M	G	N
G	P	E	I	I	D	P	C	A	B	P	Z	N	R	F
E	W	T	M	A	F	K	J	Y	V	G	I	X	D	E
Z	L	D	D	E	D	N	U	O	R	G	O	R	K	S
T	N	B	P	Q	G	O	Z	E	N	P	F	J	E	E
R	E	Y	A	R	P	I	A	A	M	K	M	C	F	H
J	Y	L	V	D	O	T	H	W	C	S	Q	A	A	U
U	L	I	E	W	N	C	O	N	S	T	A	N	T	D
D	I	B	D	E	A	E	E	N	I	W	D	F	H	N
E	C	P	S	J	F	R	P	S	E	C	U	R	E	U
C	G	S	U	S	X	I	M	E	S	I	E	Q	R	Y
Z	L	S	K	U	P	D	L	S	D	M	N	N	P	W
O	G	H	I	T	C	S	U	U	G	X	K	H	R	V

- CHANGING
- DIRECTION
- GROUNDED
- LIFE
- SAFE
- CONSTANT
- FATHER
- HAND
- PRAYER
- SECURE
- DEPENDABLE
- GREATNESS
- INSPIRE
- PROCESS
- WARM

LESSON #29

The Father Protects Us From Hurting Ourselves

Both of my girls loooove Dad's scrambled eggs. I put a little seasoning salt, a dash or two of fresh ground pepper, plenty of butter, and mix it all together with a whole ripe avocado! When the temperature of the "best eggs ever" is just right, I smash them into small bite-size pieces and feed one scoop to Johannah and another scoop to Jessica. Right now they're still young enough to eat from the same spoon without conflict; we'll see how long this lasts. After I feed them, I try to get something to eat for myself, and since I'm on a health kick right now, I eat an apple dipped in almond butter with a bottle of water. While I was sitting on the couch eating my breakfast, my bottle of water was on the floor, and I saw Jessica lock her eyes on it and set out to snag it for herself. In this scenario, it was a bottle of water, but many other times it has been juice, cups of coffee, a glass of wine, or any other liquid that could potentially stain the carpet and/or cause her harm.

As soon as she made her move, I relocated my water to a corner of the couch that was the farthest away from her. As a countermeasure, she repositioned her body and started towards it again with renewed intent. This time not only did I tuck the bottle away better, but I also put my leg in front of it to protect it and to protect her because if she got to it and tried to drink it, it could go up her nose, down her throat the wrong way, or end up all over her clothes. My leg also ensured she wouldn't spill it all over the carpet, making it damp, potentially growing mold, and overall just not being good for our environment. Now if it were something hot, more staining, or more severe to her health or the environment than water, then the need for a safeguard would become increasingly more necessary.

Our Father will also provide the necessary protection for us even when we think we'd benefit from attaining what He deems harmful to us. I'm sure many of us are thankful that God intervened and removed a damaging relationship out of our lives before it was too late or closed a door on an opportunity that we thought was appealing; in retrospect, we see how it was only a detour in disguise. Much like when God set an angel with a flaming sword in front of the tree of life to prevent Adam from disobeying Him again, Our Father will stand in the way of our temporary desires to protect us from the harm we may unknowingly bring upon ourselves. Let's embrace Our Father's protection.

NUMBERS 22:21-22A (NLT)

 So the next morning Balaam got up, saddled his donkey, and started off with the Moabite officials. But God was angry that Balaam was going, so He sent the angel of the Lord to stand in the road to block his way.

THE FATHER PROTECTS US FROM HURTING OURSELVES

E	Z	O	D	Y	M	Z	K	S	W	E	X	H	H	N
B	V	P	P	D	Z	H	D	T	A	D	V	A	D	O
O	A	R	W	Q	L	Y	A	N	D	O	O	R	D	I
P	L	F	O	D	P	Y	R	A	R	O	P	M	E	T
Z	V	X	X	H	O	D	M	N	O	N	H	F	S	N
K	Q	R	E	B	V	A	C	E	W	O	M	U	I	E
R	O	I	L	E	G	R	Z	V	S	I	W	L	R	V
O	Z	C	P	I	H	S	N	O	I	T	A	L	E	R
U	B	F	N	V	T	F	R	C	N	C	T	D	S	E
F	U	G	A	N	K	N	G	I	X	E	E	V	F	T
Y	V	S	I	T	G	D	H	R	C	T	R	A	V	N
X	N	T	S	Z	H	I	P	V	O	O	H	V	B	I
P	M	W	S	A	F	E	G	U	A	R	D	G	H	Y
C	U	F	R	M	K	P	R	F	Z	P	O	G	E	T
M	U	R	H	J	C	S	D	W	S	W	O	O	E	O

- PROTECTION
- HARMFUL
- DESIRES
- INTERVENTION
- SWORD
- COVENANT
- FATHER
- DOOR
- RELATIONSHIP
- TEMPORARY
- DAMAGING
- DETOURS
- SAFEGUARD
- WATER
- LEG

LESSON #30

Mature Children — Be Fed, Feed Yourself, Feed Others, and Serve

As a father, there are certain stages of life that I'm determined to walk my children through—certain milestones that will help indicate their level of development and maturity. For example, having two young children, a couple of those milestones are centered around food and sustaining themselves. We are now in the early phases where most of the time my wife and I have to feed them ourselves. We have to spoon them their food, siphon them their medicine, pour their drinks, and hand them snacks or else risk them being malnourished. At the moment, we are their primary source for being fed.

As a natural course in their maturation process, I'm going to want them to soon learn how to feed themselves. This is a significant area of growth for them to become self-sustaining individuals. Right now, Jessica can pincer grip some Cheerios and can put a small portion of food to her mouth and eat it. Johannah is able to bite off a chunk of banana if you hold it in front of her, and she can also drink from a bottle. So from them being fed to them feeding themselves is a progression in their childhood that I am excited to see.

At some point in their life journey, I hope they become contributing members in our larger community and learn how to teach, or feed, other people. This way they can use what they've learned and make an impact on lives beyond themselves—to be able to feed one another when they see a need and help each other out as a reliable resource. This will attest that they're living beyond their own basic desires and beyond their restricted worlds and can be there for someone else when they need sustenance. So when there's a little brother or sister for them, I'm going to want them to feed their siblings so that they can be an extension of my hand.

Lastly, since we are a benevolent household, I want them to serve. I want them to serve their parents, one another, those that are less fortunate, and those that they encounter in the world. It's a passion of mine to develop a servant's heart in them so they can appreciate life more. This way they can reflect the things that I've taught and shown them as I served, fed, and took care of them. As their father, I look for my children to be fed, feed themselves, feed others, and serve.

Sounds like a model of discipleship from Our Father for us, doesn't it? He instructs us, as His children of the light, to walk in the footsteps of Christ and produce evidence of His Kingdom here on Earth. Let's put aside our selfish ways and walk in His light, in the power of His might, and in our maturity. Let's grow into the example Our Father has set before us so the world can see by our progress and by how we serve one another that we have a loving, attentive Father.

HEBREWS 5:12–14 (NLT)

" You have been believers so long now that you ought to be teaching others. Instead, you need someone to teach you again the basic things about God's word. You are like babies who need milk and cannot eat solid food. For someone who lives on milk is still an infant and doesn't know how to do what is right. Solid food is for those who are mature, who through training have the skill to recognize the difference between right and wrong.

MATURE CHILDREN — BE FED, FEED YOURSELF, FEED OTHERS, AND SERVE

E	Z	Y	H	P	G	E	X	O	U	P	C	I	Z	S
S	L	H	S	I	F	L	E	S	X	A	U	L	X	V
D	D	W	B	H	G	J	L	U	T	Z	Y	B	H	P
R	Y	M	X	S	R	E	H	T	O	Q	W	M	R	G
E	V	I	D	E	N	C	E	H	Q	E	B	K	V	F
M	X	R	H	L	Y	N	M	Y	B	U	L	N	F	S
A	D	T	M	P	T	R	O	Z	L	D	N	X	N	F
J	A	H	E	I	I	U	D	I	Q	B	K	Y	B	E
F	F	I	V	C	R	T	G	E	N	J	D	U	G	V
W	Z	E	R	S	U	H	N	X	F	Z	T	B	C	J
Y	A	U	E	I	T	G	I	J	P	P	A	N	E	S
I	X	L	S	D	A	I	K	A	K	X	L	S	Q	L
M	F	F	K	V	M	M	E	I	M	S	Q	Y	V	I
C	U	Z	F	Q	W	W	N	J	H	G	O	T	U	A
R	M	R	I	C	I	X	H	I	L	P	U	P	O	M

- FED
- FEED
- YOURSELF
- OTHERS
- SERVE
- LIGHT
- ATTENTIVE
- FATHER
- DISCIPLESHIP
- EVIDENCE
- KINGDOM
- SELFISH
- WALK
- MIGHT
- MATURITY

LESSON #31

The Fathers Love Will Not Reinforce Your Mess

For one day a week over the course of three months, my wife and I took behavioral therapy classes for parents. We did this at first to qualify for services for my oldest daughter but also so that we can better understand what causes her to express certain behavior. In these classes, they taught us about the optimal time to care for and to attend to our children, including the times when they throw a tantrum. To illustrate this lesson, they had a diagram of a bell curve, if you can imagine it, low on one end, high in the middle, and equally low on the other end. So in short, it's low, high, low. The beginning low end of the curve represents the ramp-up of an episode, the high is when they're in full flare, and the opposite low end represents when they've finally wound down.

It's our family's night-time routine to place our children into bed anywhere between 7:30 and 8 p.m. Not coincidentally, this is when both of them, but primarily young Jessica, tend to have a fit. They're not angry because they're hungry nor because they're in pain, and it's not because of anything we've omitted to do as parents. They just don't feel like being in bed at that time and don't want to go to sleep. So nightly, at the same bat time, same bat channel, they have a fit. As much as my wife and I do not want to hear our children screaming their lungs out and experiencing what sounds to be all sorts of anguish and sorrow, our therapy classes taught us some valuable lessons about incentivizing behavior.

We've learned that if we go in there to pacify them at the height of their screaming, we are only encouraging a behavior that communicates, "If you want Mom and Dad to give you attention and come to your bedside, then please explode into a frenzied episode." Since that is not the type of behavior we intend to encourage, we do not go in their room during the peak of their outbursts, and we let them scream it out. Now when they start to calm down, we tend to walk in and check on them, making sure that their heads are not too hot, the room temperature is good, they can still breathe, and at times I'll even rub their heads and kiss them on the cheeks. I go the extra mile to let them know their father still loves them. I'm not going to encourage the mess you do to bring attention to yourself, but in the end, know that I heard you and I was aware of what was going on. As their father, it's important I reinforce behaviors that build trust, composure, and proper conduct so they can learn to be content in any and every situation.

This brings to mind a saying I've heard that reminds us that "God will not bless your mess." As Our Father, if He endorses our messy, unhealthy behavior, then it may send the wrong message that this is the type of character He shows His favor upon. As His children, our activities and behavior are direct representations of Him to the world, and Our Father does not want to be misrepresented.

Gut-check time. If you know you're out of line and not operating in the character, will, and integrity of Christ and are wondering why Our Father is not moving on your behalf, it's probably because He does not want to bless your mess. He'd rather take the time necessary to cultivate an attitude within us that honors His will and brings us closer to His temperament. When we take the time to modify our misbehavior, we will see He was always there with us, even while we were going through our most difficult situations. Then our rewarding Father will rest His hand of favor on our life. He will touch us by His Word, kiss us with His Spirit, and approve of us as a reflection of Himself for the world to witness a symbol of His fatherly love.

PSALM 119:1–8 (NLT)

" Joyful are people of integrity, who follow the instructions of the LORD. Joyful are those who obey His laws and search for Him with all their hearts. They do not compromise with evil, and they walk only in His paths. You have charged us to keep Your commandments carefully. Oh, that my actions would consistently reflect Your decrees! Then I will not be ashamed when I compare my life with Your commands. As I learn Your righteous regulations, I will thank You by living as I should! I will obey Your decrees. Please don't give up on me!

THE FATHERS LOVE WILL NOT REINFORCE YOUR MESS

V	Y	U	T	M	L	U	C	F	T	A	S	W	T	B
E	W	D	B	T	F	O	C	Z	N	T	D	P	R	W
C	G	R	G	U	N	B	V	B	N	T	S	U	R	T
T	P	P	V	D	K	E	G	E	T	I	B	Y	E	M
S	Y	B	U	C	L	Y	M	H	S	T	M	G	I	V
Y	Y	C	S	W	O	D	J	A	G	U	E	M	N	Y
O	T	M	H	A	N	M	G	V	R	D	M	C	F	T
W	P	E	B	A	H	Q	P	I	F	E	S	S	O	I
E	S	I	M	O	R	P	M	O	C	R	P	T	R	R
Q	U	M	G	T	L	A	K	R	S	S	E	M	C	G
C	O	M	P	K	R	G	C	G	A	U	L	K	E	E
C	O	Z	F	L	R	C	Q	T	D	V	R	B	Q	T
Q	F	S	W	R	C	G	R	C	E	O	B	E	C	N
Q	W	M	D	Z	Q	Y	M	Y	A	R	L	G	Z	I
B	D	B	B	L	G	J	Q	L	C	B	W	G	T	H

- REINFORCE
- MESS
- LOVE
- OBEY
- CHARACTER
- ATTITUDE
- TEMPERAMENT
- BEHAVIOR
- TRUST
- COMPOSURE
- CONDUCT
- SYMBOL
- INTEGRITY
- COMPROMISE
- COMMANDMENTS

LESSON #32

May the Lord Our Father, Turn His Face Towards You, and Give You Peace

There are times when I am with my daughters when Jessica does something—it really doesn't matter what—and she gets really excited because she knows she's grabbed my attention. She will pick up a toy and drop it, grab an empty plastic bottle and crunch it, or simply touch her sister's leg—you know the sort of gestures children think are ingenious.

What I've noticed is that after she's completed her feat, she'll quickly turn around and look at me. I can feel her bright eyes reading my facial responses for signs of praise. Since she's already thrilled with herself because she's done something really cool, funny, or silly, looking back to see me smiling at her is all a kid like her can ask for. She looks to my smile to give her approval of who she is, what she's doing, and how awesome it was. Often when I answer her with a smile, she'll return it with an even happier expression—so much so that she may start to giggle, shake, and eventually fall down in delight. She oozes an energy that screams, "Yeah! I did a really good thing. Dad saw it and smiled! Aw, man, this is the best!" Then she'll drop down, roll in a circle, laugh, and do other silly things one-year-old children do. Fun times.

Jessica's desire for my acceptance reminds me of how we are are to live a life devoted to pleasing Our Father. Practicing faith, being generous, loving difficult people, and showing mercy are a few of the ways we can live before God and get a warm-hearted grin of joy from Our Dad. It is with this intention that I pray the blessings of Numbers 6:24–26 over our lives as children of Our Heavenly Father:

NUMBERS 6:24–26 (NIV)

> The LORD bless you
> and keep you;
> the LORD make His face shine on you
> and be gracious to you;
> the LORD turn His face toward you
> and give you peace.

Our Father sees you doing your thing, and He's smiling, so live in peace.

MAY THE LORD OUR FATHER, TURN HIS FACE TOWARDS YOU, AND GIVE YOU PEACE

M	T	P	S	U	O	I	C	A	R	G	V	V	D	O
V	I	G	W	G	K	K	N	G	N	I	V	O	L	T
D	E	M	P	G	N	I	L	I	M	S	R	X	D	P
S	D	J	O	Y	T	I	S	O	R	E	N	E	G	E
F	U	N	L	K	M	A	S	P	A	G	T	K	L	G
D	E	V	O	T	E	D	P	S	U	P	Z	H	J	T
M	A	U	Z	L	Y	F	E	P	E	M	V	M	Q	I
N	A	R	P	Q	P	F	A	C	E	L	Z	J	G	D
O	B	U	U	F	T	E	C	I	I	G	B	Z	B	M
A	U	M	V	I	H	A	E	F	T	T	S	Q	I	G
R	H	N	L	V	T	P	I	L	Q	H	O	D	E	N
N	C	Q	L	K	C	E	Q	L	I	B	C	N	I	B
L	S	U	D	B	O	J	N	N	W	E	K	X	N	A
R	S	H	N	B	J	J	E	M	B	Y	E	T	F	T
H	E	E	M	D	N	N	M	L	D	J	C	L	M	M

- FACE
- PEACE
- SMILING
- FAITH
- GENEROSITY
- LOVING
- BLESSINGS
- SHINE
- GRACIOUS
- ACCEPTED
- DEVOTED
- PLEASING
- GRIN
- JOY
- NOTICED

LESSON #33
The Father Provides Everything We Need

In the mornings, I get the girls ready for the day. My wife takes care of preparing the food, bottles, and bags and places them in the refrigerator for easy grab-'n-go access. When time permits, she also gets Jessica dressed, aside from small things like socks, shoes, or a jacket, before she heads out for work. I'm totally responsible for getting Johannah dressed, and before we leave the house, I like to make sure that both of them are fully outfitted to weather any occasion. I make it a practice to slightly open the window to feel the air and look up at the sky to get a read on the clouds, and if I determine it to be even slightly cool, I add a layer to their outfits for good measure. To make things a little more inconvenient, Johannah likes to habitually kick off her shoes, and now she's taught Jessica to do the same, so when we leave the house and before they exit my car to go into daycare, I make sure they both have on jackets, socks, and shoes.

The same goes with feeding them. Depending on when we leave the house, if it's really early, I may not feed them and instead allow them to be fed at daycare by the staff. But if I have any question whether they may or may not be fed because the staff may assume, by say 8:30 a.m., they should have already eaten breakfast, then before we leave the house, I make it my duty to also feed them breakfast and give them a bottle. I'm intentional with this foresight because once they leave my hands and are out of my immediate care, I want them to have the best start possible to prepare them for any challenge the day will bring. As their father, I prepare them in such a way that they can thrive even if there is some oversight on behalf of the people I'm trusting them with.

In the same manner, I believe Our Father gives us everything we need daily to do the work He's given us to do. Each day, with new mercies, He "stocks us up" with everything we need to get through the trials, relationships, successes, and responsibilities that we may not know whether we can handle or not. Every day when we awake, He restocks our ability to withstand, He restocks our grace and mercies, and He restocks our inner man by His Holy Spirit so that before we hit the front door, Our Father has given us a portion for today that can withstand anything that the day may bring. Let's keep our faith, courage, and confidence in Him.

JOHN 16:33 (NLT)

" I have told you all this so that you may have peace in Me. Here on earth you will have many trials and sorrows. But take heart, because I have overcome the world.

THE FATHER PROVIDES EVERYTHING WE NEED

Y	Z	T	Z	D	S	Y	Q	P	H	S	C	Z	I	S
E	T	R	V	S	Z	C	C	O	W	N	H	L	S	U
G	Y	I	N	M	I	F	E	R	H	X	S	E	D	E
L	A	A	L	T	C	E	T	T	E	W	A	C	Z	E
G	D	L	S	I	K	H	D	I	U	M	W	A	F	I
R	Y	S	T	P	B	W	A	O	I	S	B	E	E	L
A	R	E	L	A	T	I	O	N	S	H	I	P	S	Y
C	E	A	Q	D	B	T	S	M	D	W	O	R	K	F
E	V	E	R	Y	T	H	I	N	G	L	X	O	C	O
Q	E	T	L	M	L	S	Z	B	O	Z	E	V	O	D
U	H	O	X	C	S	T	F	I	G	R	L	I	T	A
S	G	A	A	O	J	A	V	G	D	Y	S	D	S	M
R	G	X	A	U	V	N	P	R	Y	K	A	E	E	J
Y	F	O	E	Q	E	D	U	H	B	T	S	S	R	W
R	D	B	R	X	R	A	I	V	R	A	L	F	H	Z

- PEACE
- GIFT
- EVERYDAY
- EVERYTHING
- WORK
- RELATIONSHIPS
- TRIALS
- RESPONSIBILITY
- WITHSTAND
- RESTOCKS
- GRACE
- MERCY
- PORTION
- HANDLE
- PROVIDES

LESSON #34

It Brings the Father Joy to Hear His Children Speak His Words

Oh my little Jessica! Jessica is now learning how to repeat everything we say, and it's amazing to say the least. Not only is she repeating words but she is also a good helper bee for us these days. For example, she can get Johannah's bottle from the kitchen and bring it to her wherever she is in the house. Even more impressively, she knows the difference between what's hers (bottle, food, toys) and what belongs to Johannah.

This day Jessica was as helpful as ever as she went into the dining area and grabbed Johannah's bottle for her and brought it into the living room. But when she brought it, she accidentally carried it upside down so that it was dripping a trail of juice behind her. Upon seeing this, I gently grabbed the bottle in her hand and turned it upright while saying "up" and correcting the positioning. Jessica turned towards me and slightly tilted her head with a perplexed look on her face, and I could see she was trying to figure out what I was communicating to her.

Then, to my surprise, she turned and repeated back to me "up"! I nearly lost my mind. It was so AWESOME to hear my words come out of her mouth! It's an incredible feeling to know she's listening and communicating to me, with the little she does know, based on the words I've given her to use. Furthermore, to affirm what she's learned when she uses her words and says "up," I'd smile and turn the bottle up again.

As a parent, I get the funny feeling that down the line this "repeating thing" may need some adjustment, but for now, it made me realize how wondrous it is for a father to hear their child using the words they have given the child to speak. Instantly, it exemplifies a level of maturity and growth, and it shows a oneness of understanding that we're on the same page and talking the same talk. I'm almost certain that when she starts to grasp more of my language and I hear her say things that I've said to her, probably making requests in the same mannerisms that I've asked for them, I'll be more than happy to give her the requests she asks for.

This reminds me of how Our Father is with His children. He said in His Word, "if you remain in me and my words remain in you, ask whatever you wish, and it will be done for you" (John 15:7, NIV). Our Father delights in watching His children learn His Word. He loves hearing His children speak His Word to life's circumstances and back to Him. He takes joy in performing whatever the child is asking. Imagine the smile you put on His face when you remain in Him this way. If you desire a more fulfilling prayer life or a positive mindset throughout your day, I challenge you to speak Our Father's words to your situation and witness the difference they make.

JOHN 15:7, 16 (NIV)

"If you remain in me and my words remain in you, ask whatever you wish, and it will be done for you. You did not choose me, but I chose you and appointed you so that you might go and bear fruit—fruit that will last—and so that whatever you ask in my name the Father will give you.

IT BRINGS THE FATHER JOY TO HEAR HIS CHILDREN SPEAK HIS WORDS

N	P	C	R	S	U	W	U	R	J	C	G	Y	U	C
E	O	N	S	R	R	O	F	T	B	A	O	U	V	D
R	Z	I	F	R	O	A	L	Z	R	R	S	C	B	R
D	F	A	T	H	E	R	P	Y	W	W	Q	J	J	K
L	S	M	I	A	D	F	D	H	O	Q	T	P	X	E
I	R	E	P	V	U	W	A	Q	R	J	O	P	W	S
H	M	R	Z	L	G	T	E	S	D	N	I	M	T	K
C	R	R	F	N	E	V	I	T	I	S	O	P	U	G
S	C	I	I	V	H	K	E	S	B	P	M	J	R	R
S	L	R	E	Y	A	R	P	N	V	O	J	Y	N	R
L	B	R	K	X	D	E	U	R	H	A	O	G	D	V
A	K	H	Q	C	A	Z	R	P	E	D	X	X	I	O
I	R	G	O	K	I	L	K	A	L	N	K	U	H	N
T	U	A	S	F	L	H	R	K	P	C	V	O	M	S
K	S	A	L	N	Y	D	G	X	F	T	P	R	S	H

- BRING
- FATHER
- JOY
- CHILDREN
- SPEAK
- WORD
- DAILY
- REMAIN
- ASK
- WHATEVER
- SITUATION
- POSITIVE
- MINDSET
- FULFILL
- PRAYER

LESSON #35

Sometimes The Father Says Wait, Hold On, Stop.

Simply stated, we all know it's important to get dressed before we leave the house. I'm talking about the basics; like pants, socks, shoes, shirt and if it's cold, maybe a jacket. This is just normal, routine daily preparation. Today as I'm getting Johannah dressed I realize she wants to do other things while I'm dressing her. The problem with her being preoccupied when I'm getting her dressed is that there's an urgency for me to get them clothed and out of the house so we can get to daycare, drop them off, and I can quickly get to work at a reasonable time. So mornings for us are pretty routine, we have things to do, places to go, a fixed amount of time, and we have a couple stops to make. Those are four key parts to a successful start, and important for our lesson today.

As I'm getting them dressed Johannah wants to play, she wants to do things like grab her hair products and play with them. All the while I have to lay her back down and put on her shirt. So I tell her to, 'Hold on...' as I take care of this part of her preparation process. Then she wants to roll off of the changing table and I'm like 'Hold on...' because first, I don't want you rolling off — that's dangerous and number two I'm trying to put on your pants. Then she wants to look out of the window so I say 'Hold on...' because I'm trying to do her hair and put barrettes in it and it's difficult to do so if she doesn't keep still. Each time I found myself asking her to either 'Hold On', 'Wait' or 'Stop' with phrases like "Wait, Wait, don't do that now I have to get this done!", "Wait, Wait until I put this on", or "Johannah, why are you doing that now, Hold On!". Ultimately, I found myself routinely saying "Wait, Hold On, and Stop" and it started to make me realize something about Our Father's timing.

We may get frustrated and not know why God is saying 'Wait' instead of immediately giving us what we think we want or need. Why must we 'Hold On' for so long or so often? Why would He ask for us to 'Stop' doing certain acts that bring us the pleasure we desire? You may think He's trying to stop you from having fun, trying to stop you from the simple, enjoyable comforts of 'looking out the window' or 'rolling off the table' (if you consider risk to be alluring — even though only He knows the end of every risk) but the Father has a plan for you. He has a purpose for your life and your life has a fixed time limit, we live 'fixed-term lives' here on earth and our Father has an assignment for us to complete while we are still here. He has predestined places for us to go, and He needs us to be efficient and effective on this journey because He has purposed a couple stops for us to make along the way.

So trust Our Father when you're in His hands and He's preparing you for your day's journey. He's gearing you up for where you're going next in life and that's why He's taking the necessary preparation time now. While He's preparing you, you may want to do some things in the interim that you think are more exciting, or more adventurous, or more pleasurable with your time. But sometimes the Father will ask you to 'Wait', other times He may say 'Hold On', and then there are times He'll command you to 'Stop' to get you focused on what's most important for your journey. Let's trust the Father.

PSALM 46:10

" Be still, and know that I am God! I will be honored by every nation. I will be honored throughout the world."

SOMETIMES THE FATHER SAYS WAIT, HOLD ON, STOP.

P	H	T	I	F	K	S	W	N	E	T	J	L	M	Y
E	R	A	C	A	Q	U	Z	I	V	E	G	P	Y	D
M	Q	E	W	T	R	C	J	M	S	A	P	X	L	Y
A	F	V	S	H	Y	O	N	F	M	D	R	J	K	T
K	P	L	D	E	U	F	B	O	S	C	O	M	I	Z
X	T	O	E	R	N	Z	T	T	T	X	T	M	E	B
L	D	V	N	O	I	T	A	R	A	P	E	R	P	X
X	B	E	I	T	N	S	A	A	W	L	C	O	B	R
N	Y	Z	S	K	F	U	H	T	Y	A	T	E	M	G
K	N	S	Z	J	P	R	O	V	I	S	I	O	N	S
M	D	W	N	K	Q	T	L	V	N	O	O	T	U	K
Y	A	W	N	Q	C	M	D	K	F	B	N	U	H	K
A	K	D	B	X	T	M	Z	K	Q	W	G	Q	Y	E
S	M	Z	N	N	S	O	G	F	A	Q	F	X	L	G
F	S	X	L	V	K	J	T	L	N	P	O	L	J	Y

- CARE
- HOLD
- PREPARATION
- PROVISION
- TRUST
- FATHER
- JOURNEY
- PRESENTATION
- STOP
- WAIT
- FOCUS
- LOVE
- PROTECTION
- TIMELY
- WISDOM

LESSON #36

The Father First Wants You to Handle The Last Thing He Gave You

My children are now at the point in their lives where they want to eat some of whatever it is I'm eating. Oftentimes I'll sit against the couch on the floor of the living room and snack on something sweet or crunchy just to pass the time. When I do so, I'm quickly joined by my daughters sitting on my lap and staring directly at my mouth while I eat my refreshments. Right now Jessica has pressured her way into getting a piece of my apple, and since it's a healthy treat, I don't mind breaking her off a small bite-size chunk to enjoy with her pops. While she was working on chewing her small chunk, I continued to enjoy the rest of my apple. She then noticed that I'm eating way faster than she was and that the apple was quickly disappearing. She then turned to me with her pretty little eyes and started to press me for more of my snack. But in the process of her whining and petitioning, she opened her mouth, and I saw the same chunk of apple that I had previously given her before.

Seeing this, I said to her, "Until you finish what I gave you to eat before, you do not need any more. I'll first need to see that you can chew and swallow that first piece safely; THEN you can come to me and I'll consider giving you another portion." It's irresponsible of me as a father to give her more of what she wants, but cannot handle, as it can end up being tragic for her. In other words, let me see how you handle what I first gave you; then I can give you what you need next!

Isn't that how Our Father simultaneously provides and protects us in spite of our natural response of hoarding when faced with greed and the fear of the unknown? Even when our capacity to manage His blessings in our lives is maxed out, we still at times look to see the greater capacity of those around us and desire what they have. We forget that regardless of the quantity of Our Father's favor we or others are experiencing, when we are full, we are full. If we were to get what others have when we have not finished with what He has already given us, then we'll either waste it or overwhelm ourselves.

EXODUS 16:16–18 (NLT)

These are the LORD's instructions: "Each household should gather as much as it needs. Pick up two quarts for each person in your tent." So the people of Israel did as they were told. Some gathered a lot, some only a little. But when they measured it out, everyone had just enough. Those who gathered a lot had nothing left over, and those who gathered only a little had enough. Each family had just what it needed.

THE FATHER FIRST WANTS YOU TO HANDLE THE LAST THING HE GAVE YOU

B	J	P	M	Y	J	U	W	B	U	K	H	B	F	E
B	P	R	E	M	O	G	O	H	X	I	L	C	F	Y
O	H	O	A	P	O	K	G	L	G	O	Q	O	N	C
S	V	T	S	H	S	U	R	Z	A	T	W	E	X	P
J	V	E	U	W	O	N	J	L	T	T	E	O	B	X
Z	Q	C	R	N	T	K	U	A	H	D	E	N	E	S
C	A	T	E	W	G	F	Y	K	E	J	J	E	P	D
A	J	S	D	C	H	I	L	D	R	E	N	O	S	B
T	U	U	C	T	S	E	D	I	V	O	R	P	G	R
C	P	S	I	Q	Q	P	L	E	N	T	Y	F	Q	D
R	Q	A	Z	F	Z	B	R	M	I	T	F	N	J	J
U	F	X	D	R	K	Y	R	O	G	E	T	N	J	F
R	U	N	K	N	O	W	N	R	V	G	V	G	U	M
N	C	X	N	N	K	V	U	S	P	A	E	I	X	X
S	J	C	E	T	L	T	I	C	I	N	F	B	D	A

- CHILDREN
- ENOUGH
- PROVIDES
- PROTECTS
- PORTION
- PLENTY
- OVERWHELM
- FAVOR
- OMER
- MEASURED
- NEEDED
- GATHER
- EVERYONE
- FAITHFUL
- UNKNOWN

LESSON #37

Our Worship Grabs the Father's Heart

We have two bishops in our church family; one is our Senior Pastor/Teacher, Bishop Kenneth C. Ulmer, and the second is the Pastor of Discipleship Care, Bishop Sheridan McDaniel. Bishop McDaniel previously pastored another church, called the Worship Center. Today, his ministry continues to have a strong emphasis on worship in the house of the Lord.

Currently, I am the Pastor of Young Adults (affectionately called Twenty20), and we recently had a young adult leadership retreat where Bishop Sheridan came and taught on personal worship and gave us an exercise to complete each night. This exercise was for us to get on our knees and lift both hands in the air while singing a song to God each night before we went to sleep and each morning when we first arose. The song could be any song we knew as the intent of the song was to set an atmosphere of reflection and gratitude. Once the atmosphere was set, we were to say a prayer to God. So in this exercise, we started the day on our knees, hands up and arms stretched above our heads, singing a song and saying a prayer, and then we'd close the day in the same manner.

My daughter Johannah is going on three years old, and she's still not yet walking. When I first step foot into the house from work and she sees me, or if she sees me about to leave the house, she will crawl over to my feet and position herself directly in front of me. With her eyes locked on mine, she will lift up on her knees and hold her hands up towards me, indicating she wants me to pick her up (and hold her, hug her, do all that fun stuff that we love to do) and possibly take her with me. When she crawls to me, it takes her some time to reach me, so I can see her gradually getting closer; then I can see her getting ready to lift up, so I stay completely still because she may need my legs to help support her as she raises. I figure if she's taken the time to crawl over to me, to situate herself on her knees, and lift her arms up to me because she wants me to lift her, then I will do anything I can do to help her reach me. And since I know she wants me to hug her and hold her and love on her, then as soon as she is in position with her arms up, I reach right down, scoop her up, and kiss all over her face (she likes how my beard tickles her neck). I squeeze her tight, and I love on her.

Likewise, there is something special about being at Our Father's feet. When we get into a position of surrender, a position of need and dependence, and a position of relationship, love grabs Our Father's heart and bends Him towards us. It causes Him to respond with love and acknowledgment and for Him to pick us up when we need Him most and bring us closer to Himself. Let's worship the Lord in a way that demonstrates our total dependence on Him.

JOHN 4:23 (NLT)

> But the time is coming—indeed it's here now—when true worshipers will worship the Father in spirit and in truth. The Father is looking for those who will worship Him that way.

OUR WORSHIP GRABS THE FATHER'S HEART

K	O	O	X	W	G	O	V	K	N	B	P	O	B	V
M	Q	W	Q	Q	N	I	E	T	C	O	N	V	Y	P
Y	H	Z	N	B	Q	Y	S	Q	L	O	N	E	X	A
J	K	I	R	P	I	H	S	R	O	W	Z	A	E	J
D	M	F	V	W	P	T	S	Y	S	W	X	Z	T	J
H	E	B	S	J	R	J	Q	I	E	T	G	B	U	J
C	U	P	L	A	O	Y	J	V	N	R	F	E	C	I
J	Z	M	E	X	V	C	O	M	E	G	O	S	Q	G
C	S	H	B	N	I	L	B	D	S	G	C	S	S	R
J	R	Y	W	L	D	L	N	T	S	E	R	E	F	Y
M	Z	B	F	T	E	E	F	D	B	D	M	A	H	A
J	S	W	Q	T	R	W	N	E	Z	C	T	A	B	Q
A	Y	W	D	R	T	D	H	C	H	H	A	N	D	S
Q	B	G	U	I	G	L	P	U	E	L	I	W	O	R
C	J	S	Y	G	S	U	D	R	I	L	V	M	I	Y

- WORSHIP
- GRABS
- FATHER
- HEART
- SURRENDER
- HUMBLE
- FEET
- DWELL
- REST
- LOVE
- CLOSENESS
- DEPENDENCE
- PROVIDER
- HANDS
- SING

LESSON #38

The Father's War Cry

One thing I've learned in my few years of trying to be the father God has called me to be is that during really tough times, my war cry sounds a lot like my desperate plea. At the end of the day, the determining factor if you hear a roar or a whimper depends on who's listening and if you're for me or against me. If you're the enemy, you need to be afraid because I'm resolved and fully convinced that the work God has started in me He is faithful to complete, regardless of the failures and setbacks I have experienced. When you hear my thunderous shout, take heed that there is no turning back for me. I've given my life to Him, and I'll die pressing forward past my inner demons, past my insecurities, and past my horrible thoughts because I have decided that I'm all His.

But now if you're my Father listening, I know You can clearly hear that in my holler is a humble cry. Through it, You can pick up my heart singing, "I need You more and more during each passing moment." I believe You hear me praying for You to be here with me because there are some things in my life that are not yet settled, and I know You are able to conquer them.

I've learned that the tears in my eyes will never stop the fight in me. It's also an oversight to think I'm weak just because I'm crying. Tears are going to do what tears do; they are an emotional response. I'm not sure why they fall sometimes, but they won't stop me from suiting up and taking my position in life's battles. Tears don't stop us from getting the work done or from running strong towards the victory that our Great King has set before us. So if you see me weeping, don't let my tears fool you. As a matter of fact, you may need to let some tears flow yourself so you can blare out your war cry loud and be free. Don't let the fear of a few tears hold you back. Your worship time before Our Father should be heartfelt, with a warrior's intensity, and able to shake the enemy's ranks. Our Father is for you in this battle, so there is nothing that can stand against you. Give it a shot. Let's hear your war cry!

PSALM 18:6 (NIV)

 In my distress I called to the LORD; I cried to my God for help. From His temple He heard my voice; my cry came before Him, into His ears.

THE FATHER'S WAR CRY

R	A	Y	Y	Q	U	P	P	Y	Z	S	K	E	V	L
S	L	R	W	H	N	H	M	X	U	T	R	Y	P	R
E	C	O	N	Q	U	E	R	O	I	R	R	A	W	Y
L	J	A	J	O	N	G	E	F	V	O	I	C	E	D
L	B	R	K	E	Y	B	P	L	T	N	G	E	F	T
C	D	R	K	Q	D	C	M	C	T	G	A	I	U	E
Z	A	P	O	S	I	T	I	O	N	T	G	R	B	I
B	J	Z	T	W	Z	V	H	E	B	K	A	I	N	C
I	J	A	Y	L	Q	Y	W	G	D	E	O	B	P	X
Z	N	H	P	R	O	C	O	B	I	E	J	X	V	O
D	K	E	Y	V	Z	V	C	A	N	F	B	G	L	B
G	L	U	H	Z	E	V	R	K	O	G	C	J	B	Q
P	M	L	V	H	T	U	P	U	Z	Z	J	P	G	H
J	Y	K	I	W	U	G	D	V	A	O	P	S	A	R
Z	P	N	C	A	J	L	P	Z	O	H	F	W	V	Q

- ROAR
- WHIMPER
- WAR
- CRY
- TEARS
- FIGHT
- BATTLE
- CONQUER
- POSITION
- VICTORY
- STRONG
- WARRIOR
- VOICE
- STAND
- ENEMY

LESSON #39

The Father Gives You What's Best for You

I was sitting with Johannah and noticed that she had been sucking her thumb so much that a callus had formed on it. So I researched online and found a nail coating I can put on her thumb that will make her not want to suck her thumb any longer. This is an important prevention for us and more than just a cosmetic one because Johannah crawls on the ground at school, where other people walk, and then she puts her hand in her mouth, causing her to get sick often. In my attempt to put a stop to this thumb-sucking business, I placed a clear, nasty-tasting, child-friendly coating on her thumb that disgusts her but seems to work at stopping the behavior at times.

Like clockwork, as soon as Jessica saw me putting something on Johannah's nails, here she comes, whining, begging, and signaling for me to do the same for her. With the polish still in my hands, I turned to Jessica and said, "You don't know what you're asking me for, and if I gave you what you're asking of me, you will be **distraught** to say the least."

Then it came to me. It is a sign of immaturity to want something that someone else has, especially if you don't know if you get it, it will be to your own demise. Therefore it is in our spiritual maturity that we trust that what Our Father has assigned for us to do, given us to manage, or allowed us to have is meant specifically for us. Conversely, we must equally trust that what He has not given us to have is a part of His wisdom, protection, and sovereignty in our lives. We don't know the details, drama, stress, or concerns that come with the "blessings" we see on our friends' social media highlights. Nor are we privy to sacrifices endured when envying the casual successes overheard in our daily conversations.

Quite often we are ignorant to the bitterness of the responsibility that comes with craving the items others have. My brothers, don't compare or covet. When letting Our Father know what you want, trust He understands your needs, and make it a practice to be grateful for what He has already given you.

PHILIPPIANS 4:6–7 (NLT)

> Don't worry about anything; instead, pray about everything. Tell God what you need, and thank Him for all He has done. Then you will experience God's peace, which exceeds anything we can understand. His peace will guard your hearts and minds as you live in Christ Jesus.

THE FATHER GIVES YOU WHAT'S BEST FOR YOU

A	O	D	T	R	Q	G	P	M	H	L	I	E	W	X
O	M	W	W	Z	M	U	U	D	H	J	C	U	Z	S
N	Y	A	G	X	S	A	Y	A	R	Z	D	N	K	G
E	O	H	R	U	O	R	I	I	N	Z	J	S	E	T
X	B	I	A	D	V	D	L	U	V	F	N	N	R	D
H	P	S	T	R	E	S	S	L	E	R	B	U	I	U
O	R	D	E	C	R	T	P	M	Y	L	S	X	F	B
M	R	K	F	F	E	C	A	E	P	T	Y	T	B	U
M	A	T	U	R	I	T	Y	I	R	Q	L	W	D	S
F	O	V	L	J	G	V	O	A	L	U	V	L	N	V
M	P	D	C	O	N	C	E	R	N	S	A	Q	J	H
G	F	J	S	E	H	H	J	X	P	O	W	E	R	I
W	S	A	Y	I	G	V	T	P	B	M	D	Y	U	E
L	Z	B	Q	T	W	I	N	Y	S	S	P	J	U	S
Z	C	K	Y	Q	L	N	A	B	I	S	J	R	T	X

- ENVY
- MATURITY
- TRUST
- WISDOM
- PROTECTION
- SOVEREIGN
- DETAILS
- DRAMA
- STRESS
- CONCERNS
- GRATEFUL
- GUARDS
- HEARTS
- PEACE
- POWER

LESSON #40

Childlike Complaining Can Cause You to Miss the Father's Blessings

Have you ever watched sports, particularly basketball, when an athlete attempts to make a basket and gets fouled but the referee doesn't call the foul? Then, in an outrage over the officials' oversight, the athlete begins to complain and goes into a frenzy because they didn't get the call they wanted. Meanwhile, the other team has the ball and is already past halfcourt and about to score because the person that is supposed to be playing defense is still at the other end of the court complaining.

Well, this morning I was feeding my daughters our favorite breakfast meal: buttered eggs by Dad. I was feeding them both at the same time by toggling between the two, and this particular time, when I picked up a spoonful of eggs to give to Johannah, Jessica started to complain. She began to churn out her whiny, complaining cry because appaarently she wanted it to be her turn to eat again. She didn't like how I was not satisfying her immediate request but was giving more food to her sister.

Now, while I was feeding Johannah, Jessica went full sail into her complaining episode. She complained so long while looking at Johannah chew her food that I had already picked up another scoop of eggs to give to her, but she couldn't see what I had for her because her face was turned towards Johannah in dissatisfaction. It was remarkable for me to see how in her whining and complaining about what she didn't have and what her sister did have, she was blinded from seeing what I had made available for her now.

This makes me think about our attitudes towards one another and to Our Father. We let comparisons and complaining prevent us from seeing what Our Father has in store for us because our eyes are fixed on things that have not been prepared for us. I pray that we practice gratitude for the things we already have and are grateful for others and the things they have been given too. It may just take you letting go of your comparisons for you to realize that Our Father is ready to give you more than you were expecting. Don't let complaining make you miss Our Father's blessings for you.

PHILIPPIANS 2:13–15 (NLT)

 For God is working in you, giving you the desire and the power to do what pleases Him. Do everything without complaining and arguing, so that no one can criticize you. Live clean, innocent lives as children of God, shining like bright lights in a world full of crooked and perverse people.

CHILDLIKE COMPLAINING CAN CAUSE YOU TO MISS THE FATHER'S BLESSINGS

X	C	H	T	M	X	D	G	S	E	P	F	G	K	K
P	O	B	N	G	F	N	F	I	S	S	J	D	W	C
A	M	E	E	Z	I	L	A	E	R	B	Q	W	E	H
E	P	Q	V	E	U	X	T	E	G	W	Z	X	R	R
E	A	P	E	Q	V	O	H	F	T	Q	Y	X	G	R
C	R	S	R	N	I	T	E	T	S	D	G	P	C	T
I	I	M	P	E	O	E	R	G	K	A	R	C	N	R
T	S	Q	K	E	C	K	N	E	Y	F	A	A	C	D
C	O	M	P	L	A	I	N	I	N	G	T	Y	U	Y
A	N	A	L	P	S	L	A	E	K	H	I	I	V	H
R	S	H	O	S	E	D	U	T	I	T	T	A	R	G
P	A	T	E	Z	M	L	T	B	E	W	U	E	M	F
R	F	L	D	W	H	I	N	I	N	G	D	F	X	Y
W	B	M	Z	K	Q	H	E	N	C	Z	E	V	S	Q
E	Z	E	Q	N	K	C	T	S	Y	C	U	F	V	W

- CHILDLIKE
- ATTITUDES
- COMPARISONS
- COMPLAINING
- WHINING
- PREVENT
- SEEING
- FATHER
- PLAN
- PRACTICE
- GRATITUDE
- APPRECIATE
- OTHERS
- REALIZE
- BLESSINGS

LESSON #41

Consistently Checking in With the Father

Each time our family arrives at a new place or enters into a new environment, Jessica likes to stay really close to me. She likes to either have me pick her up and hold her or she'll stand between my legs and try to hide behind me. But the longer we stay in a locale, her curiosity will gradually take over and she'll begin to become interested in the surroundings around her. Soon after, I can see her getting antsy to wander and explore.

When she first veers off to investigate her new surroundings, she will take a few steps, turn around, and look me in the eyes as if to ask, "Is this okay, Daddy?" I'll quickly say with a slight nod and smile, "You're all right." Then she'll continue to take about three or four more steps, turn around, and check in with me with another eye-to-eye connection conveying, "Hey, is this all right, Daddy?" Again, I'll look at her and say with a nod, "You're okay." This dance of distance and permission will continue for another round or two, but then she'll figure she's gone far enough for now and will come running back into my arms. Excited about her boldness to roam, I'll pick her up, rub her head, and affirm her that she's doing a good thing.

After a brief celebration, she'll turn back around knowing she's already covered a great distance and walk confidently in the spaces she previously traveled. This time, instead of checking in after every few steps, she'll only glance at me from time to time. When she reaches the farthest point she's ever been away from me, and before going any farther, she will again turn and get another eye-to-eye confirmation from me that it's okay.

This approval process also applies if she's interested in picking up a new toy or playing with a chair; if she wants to touch it, she'll look at me. Even though she's still nonverbal, she uses her eyes to check in with her father to make sure that at each new step in her journey, I am pleased with her actions.

I think it's important as children of Our Heavenly Father that we keep our eyes on Him. Before we stray too far with our best-laid plans or move too fast in our pursuit of success, we should make it a priority to pray, meditate, and seek His face. There is another level of confidence, protection, and drive that comes from knowing we are in Our Father's good graces. It is His purpose for our lives that should determine our course of action and not the other way around. As such, it's essential we check in with Him often to know we're heading in the right direction and to experience the joy of His confirmation.

PSALM 16:8 (NIV)

I keep my eyes always on the LORD. With Him at my right hand, I will not be shaken.

CONSISTENTLY CHECKING IN WITH THE FATHER

O	D	T	N	E	M	N	O	R	I	V	N	E	H	F
V	W	P	R	O	T	E	C	T	I	O	N	U	E	X
D	H	W	V	C	I	F	G	X	I	R	Y	W	A	R
L	P	F	V	M	D	T	R	T	Z	X	P	F	V	U
L	R	J	C	V	N	W	A	O	M	K	P	I	E	N
O	E	D	N	P	E	M	C	R	W	L	U	C	N	S
W	H	R	R	U	R	X	E	H	B	U	N	O	L	J
M	T	N	O	I	S	S	I	M	R	E	P	N	Y	W
G	A	O	F	L	V	M	O	R	D	O	L	N	S	W
A	F	N	E	X	P	E	R	I	E	N	C	E	F	T
Z	O	J	N	C	N	X	F	F	S	C	M	C	C	V
C	K	J	G	B	E	N	E	F	A	N	I	T	M	L
W	K	K	Q	Q	O	F	U	A	E	D	I	I	W	T
T	F	F	B	C	F	A	N	D	L	I	B	O	N	C
S	J	O	H	L	J	A	U	K	P	M	D	N	J	G

- EXPLORE
- ENVIRONMENT
- PERMISSION
- AFFIRM
- CONNECTION
- CELEBRATION
- CONFIRMATION
- HEAVENLY
- FATHER
- PLEASED
- CONFIDENCE
- PROTECTION
- DRIVE
- EXPERIENCE
- GRACE

LESSON #42

As the Father Has Provided Before, He Will Provide for You Again

Today I was getting Johannah dressed and prepared for the day, so I had her on the changing table and was putting lotion on her body and brushing her teeth. I could see out of the corner of my eye that Jessica was getting anxious and ready for me to wrap things up so we could go eat. Soon thereafter, Jessica started to whine then cry, and then began to pull on my leg. After a short while I turned to her and said, "Hey, every day I get you dressed, then I sit you down and get Johannah dressed, then I sit her down and we all go into the living room and eat our eggs together. Today's no different. As soon as I'm done with Johannah, we're going to go in there, and we're all going to eat breakfast. So there's no need to worry; there's no need to sweat. You've seen day after day how I've done it before, and because I've done it for you before, you should know I will do it again. I know you don't always see how I'm going to do it, but that's because you have short-term memory." She does have short-term memory, but that's okay because she's a child, so I had to let her know, "Calm down; I'll take care of you. I've done it before, and I'll do it again. And I'm going to take care of you today."

I think that's a lot like how our Father feels when caring for us with our short-term memories and unnecessarily urgent prayer requests. Because we don't have absolute control of our days and have to depend upon Him, we question if He's going to provide for us again. We act as if we don't know if He's going to come through for us again, whether He hears our prayers, or if He's concerned with our hearts' troubles. The truth is if we take time to think about all He has done for us, we'll have more than enough evidence to know He's both capable and reliable. Our Father desires that we remember our testimony, that we remember where

He's brought us from, and that we look at our past experiences to see He's been there every step of the way. He reminds us if He's brought us through a hard time before, then no matter what we're facing right now, He's able to bring us through this too. Let's let the track record of Our Father's provision comfort us in times of worry and uncertainty.

PHILIPPIANS 4:19 (NLT)

> And this same God who takes care of me will supply all your needs from His glorious riches, which have been given to us in Christ Jesus.

AS THE FATHER HAS PROVIDED BEFORE, HE WILL PROVIDE FOR YOU AGAIN

P	H	V	L	K	W	R	F	Q	B	T	G	U	T	K
J	I	H	C	F	V	T	M	B	N	B	O	A	G	N
T	Y	H	B	I	U	T	G	G	Q	N	G	Q	R	G
W	N	Z	S	Q	X	D	D	C	U	Y	S	Z	T	G
T	F	U	P	N	F	X	S	R	T	N	Y	E	T	F
E	U	E	R	N	O	I	S	I	V	O	R	P	J	R
Q	X	P	O	Y	E	I	Y	R	O	M	E	M	F	P
H	H	Y	V	K	L	K	T	G	D	I	T	Z	R	X
O	T	U	E	L	B	P	A	C	T	T	D	A	A	R
B	N	R	N	I	A	G	A	N	L	S	Y	A	U	O
V	E	C	N	E	I	R	E	P	X	E	H	O	Q	W
V	G	I	L	B	U	O	R	T	R	O	H	O	H	S
K	R	F	Y	V	E	N	K	O	A	W	Z	S	J	F
Y	U	Y	R	T	R	U	S	T	R	R	O	N	F	U
C	I	Q	Q	Y	F	C	Y	X	O	L	A	S	L	F

- TROUBLES
- PRAYERS
- URGENT
- SHORT
- TERM
- MEMORY
- TRUST
- PROVISION
- RELATIONSHIP
- EXPERIENCE
- TESTIMONY
- RELIABLE
- PROVEN
- AGAIN
- CAPABLE
- RELIABLE

LESSON #43

The Father Knows Your Unique Cry

My little girls occasionally cry. As their father and a primary caregiver, it's incumbent upon me to appropriately respond to their cries to ensure I am providing them the best parental care possible. Moreover, as an attentive father who has heard them cry many times over the years, I am able to distinguish between the slight subtleties that characterize their various calls for help and/or attention. I'm always in close proximity to my girls, but during their everyday playtime around the house, I may not be directly focused on them. So being able to discern their need for help is vitally important for me. This way, I can recognize if their cries are an indication that I need to come dashing to their aid or if it's a whiny complaint that things are not going their way. Therefore if I hear them ringing out a whimpering fuss, I know to keep listening, but I can continue what I'm doing because they're going to be all right. But if I hear a primal scream that's seemingly coming from a source of pain, intense discomfort, hunger, or thirst, then I'll come running to their rescue without delay.

This revealed to me that when we complain to Our Father or gripe to Him about how we don't like what life is showing us, we can be assured He hears us even when we don't get the responses we think He should provide. Some of the discomforts we complain about in life are just because we don't like not having our way, but that's okay—we're big enough to work through a little disappointment; just give it time. However, when you're in earnest need of His help and the Father hears your desperate cry, there is nothing in this world that can stop Him from being there with you and making all things well.

PSALM 34:17 (NIV)

> The righteous cry out, and the LORD hears them; He delivers them from all their troubles.

THE FATHER KNOWS YOUR UNIQUE CRY

T	V	J	C	N	S	R	D	W	I	O	D	B	O	S
L	A	H	Y	O	R	E	E	I	P	S	M	D	T	R
M	O	C	A	R	E	S	T	O	R	E	S	J	R	L
D	N	W	C	S	V	P	A	A	C	K	H	L	R	Q
B	N	W	V	H	I	O	R	N	R	Y	A	P	C	Z
D	J	A	U	G	L	N	E	E	Y	E	T	B	P	P
W	N	V	C	A	E	D	P	N	H	Y	B	S	J	F
X	A	D	U	A	D	S	S	N	E	T	S	I	L	R
G	W	K	R	M	G	C	E	K	S	Y	A	W	L	A
S	Y	Z	Y	Q	A	R	D	P	W	T	I	F	O	O
D	W	U	K	E	U	Q	I	N	U	K	X	N	F	N
N	B	L	C	W	X	M	V	Q	Q	U	N	U	W	J
C	B	B	Z	Z	K	N	O	W	S	S	N	N	V	X
X	W	R	A	A	I	C	R	K	Z	K	G	D	M	V
M	I	K	T	U	J	Q	P	K	E	P	C	S	H	H

- FATHER
- KNOWS
- LISTENS
- CARES
- UNIQUE
- CRY
- ALWAYS
- NEAR
- PROVIDES
- DELIVERS
- HEAL
- RESTORES
- LIBERATES
- DESPERATE
- RESPONDS

LESSON #44

I Want to Be Where the Father Is

I have two little girlies, Johannah and Jessica, and you just gotta love them—they are so cute. Given they are girls and I was raised the oldest son of three boys, I am probably a little rough when I play with them. Not like extreme rough—I'm not tackling or hurting them or anything—but I do toss them, and since I have a prickly beard, when I kiss them on their faces, my beard pokes them and they can't escape. I love to bounce them up and down and all around on the couch and to squeeze them really tight, so if it's tight to me, then it's probably super duper tight to them. All in all, it just seems like my way of showing love can be interpreted as being, well, kind of rough.

My wife, on the other hand, is really soft and gentle with them. But my oldest, Johannah, likes all my rough stuff because she likes certain sensory inputs like proprioception and vestibular. These are two of the seven senses (I know, all this time we were taught about only FIVE senses right?!) my wife and I learned a lot about because of my daughter's rare diagnosis called pachygyria. These two senses primarily handle how we understand our bodies' position in space (proprioception) and our sense of spatial orientation/balance (vestibular), essentially all the feelings that go berserk while riding a roller coaster. She loves that stuff.

Since I give Johannah stimulation with my rough play, she kind of gravitates towards me, and because Jessica doesn't need that much stimulation and just wants to be treated like the little butterfly she is, she tends to gravitate towards my wife's gentleness. I say all that to say this: Whenever my wife enters or exits the room, Jessica goes right after her. Jessica is like her little "mini-me." As soon as my wife leaves, there Jessica goes; as soon as my wife returns, here comes Jessica too. Wherever my wife is, Jessica wants to be right there.

That reminds me of how our hearts should be for Our Father: Wherever He is, is where we should want to be. He knows us well enough to know how we need to be stimulated. Our trust should rest in knowing that wherever He takes us is a place we can be safe with Him and learn new things about ourselves in the process. Say this prayer with me: "Lord, I want to be where You are. I want to go where You go, and I want to be by Your side in all areas of life. Don't let me get too far from You. Wherever You decide to move, I want to be right there where You are. Amen."

PSALM 32:8 (NLT)

  The LORD says, "I will guide you along the best pathway for your life. I will advise you and watch over you."

I WANT TO BE WHERE THE FATHER IS

R	H	X	U	J	V	S	E	A	Q	M	F	K	N	T
L	G	L	W	W	P	K	L	Q	D	O	L	T	Z	Q
S	W	O	V	O	X	T	C	K	M	V	U	X	G	M
L	R	R	A	C	R	W	S	A	F	E	L	D	W	T
G	E	P	N	M	D	S	X	I	Z	J	O	L	L	X
M	H	A	U	J	E	V	I	U	F	H	F	K	U	P
M	T	L	R	N	S	G	Q	J	C	R	M	S	O	B
S	E	R	E	N	I	T	Y	E	L	R	G	N	O	J
O	G	N	E	R	R	T	C	S	Z	D	G	Q	E	U
W	O	M	W	D	E	A	E	D	R	W	O	W	J	H
A	T	R	U	V	E	Y	G	D	M	X	D	T	C	C
P	Q	B	R	P	H	E	A	R	T	T	N	O	T	B
J	Z	Z	W	L	O	I	M	R	J	E	O	Y	G	M
A	O	S	L	J	L	H	U	E	P	V	U	Q	Z	W
Z	A	B	A	Y	Y	K	K	H	R	M	A	D	P	F

- DAILY
- DESIRE
- LEARN
- GROW
- TOGETHER
- UNITED
- HOLY
- ONENESS
- HEART
- PRAYER
- PEACE
- SERENITY
- REDEEMER
- SAFE
- MOVE

LESSON #45

The Father Loves to See His Children Using the Gifts He Gave Them

God has given me the ability to play the tambourine, which is such an awkward gift for a heterosexual man. Furthermore, for some, playing the tambourine in a church service is loud, annoying, uncalled for, and disruptive, and they'd rather not have any other accompaniment to the music already coming from the church musicians. Looking around, I can see both positive and negative reactions from different people in the crowd when they hear me begin to play. I've learned to not take offense to those who don't like it; after all, I understand the clashes and clangs, bangs and pops, and accentuated beats are "just not normal." Beyond that, seeing a man playing it just takes this oddity to another level.

But God has required me to play my tambourine as a symbol of praise and of me saying "thank you" to Him for all He has done for me. Truthfully, He's the one who asks me to bring it and who calls on me to play. If I don't hear from Him, it's not uncommon for me not to carry it or even play it, although I have it with me. But when I am playing, I get the feeling He's sitting on His throne smiling, listening, and saying, "Play that tambourine, son." So regardless of how I feel about it, regardless of how I look, and regardless of how some people may find it out of place that I have a tambourine, when the Lord moves on my heart to play, I play. I play it so much at church that it's typical to see my girls sitting in my lap playing it with me.

Recently, I walked into my living room and saw my daughter Johannah beating on the tambourine. She's only three, and she doesn't know much about what she's doing with it. But since I'm a tambourine player and I love the sound, the effort, and the curiosity of the instrument, seeing her play it, I cheered her on, "Play that tambourine, girl!" and she just kept on banging it. Then I stirred her up even more by saying, "Play it for Daddy, girl!" and she just kept on banging it even louder. The more she played it, in spite of how uncoordinated, non-rhythmic, and random the sounds were, each time she banged it, I smiled because I love the sound of my girl playing that tambourine. I love the fact that she's getting lost in her own flutter and that she's familiar with this sound because of her time spent with Dad. Watching her warms my heart.

How beautiful it must be for Our Father to experience the joy of us using the gifts, abilities, skills, talents, and anointing He's given us for His pleasure. What delight it must bring Him for us when, in our own special way, we unashamedly operate in them for our audience of One. Our gifts were not intended to be kept for ourselves but to equip God's people, to do His work, and to build up the church (Ephesians 4:12 NLT). Let's magnify the goodness of Our Father with whatever ability we have so we can bring Him joy, glory, praise, and a smile when He sees us using what's He's given us for Him. Let Him use you, children.

PSALM 150 (NLT)

Praise the LORD!
Praise God in his sanctuary;
　　praise him in his mighty heaven!
Praise him for his mighty works;
　　praise his unequaled greatness!
Praise him with a blast of the ram's horn;
　　praise him with the lyre and harp!
Praise him with the tambourine and dancing;
　　praise him with strings and flutes!
Praise him with a clash of cymbals;
　　praise him with loud clanging cymbals.
Let everything that breathes sing praises to the LORD!
Praise the LORD!

THE FATHER LOVES TO SEE HIS CHILDREN USING THE GIFTS HE GAVE THEM

S	E	K	W	N	Y	L	X	H	D	K	B	P	G	T
W	E	Q	Y	P	Q	P	L	E	A	S	U	R	E	O
E	N	I	R	U	O	B	M	A	T	V	M	A	G	E
T	H	E	T	P	C	A	N	T	S	A	J	I	Q	R
G	F	K	O	I	H	N	B	L	J	B	R	S	L	K
K	A	J	Z	S	L	O	L	U	A	C	U	E	H	E
T	I	Y	A	R	N	I	Q	Q	Z	T	W	M	P	F
Y	X	N	T	U	K	N	B	L	M	L	Z	X	B	O
U	U	Y	M	S	D	T	E	A	Z	X	F	O	K	D
F	N	P	D	E	L	I	G	H	T	H	S	T	O	R
V	L	F	Z	S	T	N	E	L	A	T	N	Q	Y	D
F	S	S	T	F	I	G	V	N	O	K	Z	Y	P	V
T	P	E	Y	F	D	M	K	N	C	R	W	I	A	S
J	Q	T	Y	Q	O	P	W	U	W	E	Y	M	V	C
S	A	H	X	Z	I	F	N	V	S	N	V	X	E	M

- PRAISE
- GIFTS
- ABILITIES
- SKILLS
- TALENTS
- ANOINTING
- TAMBOURINE
- PLEASURE
- UNASHAMED
- OPERATE
- DELIGHT
- AUDIENCE
- MAGNIFY
- GLORY
- SMILE

LESSON #46

You Will Find Rest in the Father's Arms

Sometimes, late at night, I'll hold my daughters in my arms while they're sleeping and just look at them. Often they'll adjust their position just a little because they want to get into the right spot as they're being held. Just looking at them, I can see they have complete trust and comfort as they rest in my arms. Even though I have not said a word or revealed my identity in any other way, they are at peace knowing they are in their father's arms. There's safety, assurance, contentment, protection, provision, care, and love in their father's arms. I pray that your trust in Our Father is just the same. Take rest in His arms this week by speaking this promise over your life each morning and evening.

PSALM 23 (NLT)

> The LORD is my shepherd;
>   I have all that I need.
> He lets me rest in green meadows;
>   he leads me beside peaceful streams.
> He renews my strength.
> He guides me along right paths,
>   bringing honor to his name.
> Even when I walk
>   through the darkest valley,
> I will not be afraid,
>   for you are close beside me.
> Your rod and your staff
>   protect and comfort me.
> You prepare a feast for me
>   in the presence of my enemies.
> You honor me by anointing my head with oil.
>   My cup overflows with blessings.
> Surely your goodness and unfailing love will pursue me
>   all the days of my life,
> and I will live in the house of the LORD
>   forever.

YOU WILL FIND REST IN THE FATHER'S ARMS

U	K	E	E	F	F	O	C	W	N	J	A	R	Y	Q
M	V	C	V	L	U	D	A	P	E	D	D	E	A	W
F	H	A	O	O	L	E	I	R	H	N	R	V	Y	C
A	V	E	L	M	R	M	S	O	L	A	E	E	F	U
N	K	P	E	L	F	H	N	T	P	N	O	R	S	W
K	G	M	W	K	E	O	V	E	R	F	L	O	W	T
Q	M	Q	W	P	R	Y	R	C	Y	E	U	F	J	A
S	U	R	H	L	S	P	I	T	V	W	N	Y	H	Z
M	G	E	M	Q	S	S	E	N	D	O	O	G	I	R
O	R	K	B	P	P	E	W	T	L	W	U	T	T	Q
D	Q	Y	T	E	N	C	Z	O	N	I	Y	H	L	H
S	A	P	J	R	H	J	G	P	D	D	H	K	O	C
E	S	C	I	F	W	D	Z	E	K	E	W	B	H	G
J	K	Y	L	W	A	Z	X	V	L	H	M	U	Q	N
M	Y	Z	E	V	P	N	Q	V	M	V	A	Z	Z	V

- SHEPHERD
- REST
- PEACE
- RENEW
- STRENGTH
- GUIDE
- HONOR
- VALLEY
- PROTECT
- COMFORT
- PREPARE
- OVERFLOW
- GOODNESS
- LOVE
- FOREVER

LESSON #47

The Father Helps You Do What You Can't Do Alone

Johannah knows she cannot suck her thumb around me, and as trivial as that may seem to someone that doesn't have a problem like hers, as her father, I can see she struggles with this temptation. Today when I was changing her, and the changing table is about chest height so I can see everything she does in great detail, I could see her just staring at her hand, ready to enjoy her thumb like a teenage boy looking longingly at his father's car keys. I could see her grab her thumb with her opposite hand as if to say both "Get away from me" and "Come closer to me." She was caught in the classic web of "the spirit is willing but the body is weak."

I can relate to her in the struggle of wanting to do something that I should not do, and it reminds me of Paul when he said, "I want to do what is good, but I don't. I don't want to do what is wrong, but I do it anyway" (Rom. 7:15 NLT) Watching her reminds me that as children, we are in this struggle together, and we must deny the daily lure of disobedience so we can master ourselves or else we may suffer the consequences of our wrongdoing. So to ease her conflict, I gave her a toy, which she gladly starting playing with, and it took her mind off of her thumb.

Our Father also promises to provide a way for us to flee when the seduction of sin runs high. I pray, like Johannah, we are wise in our moment of temptation and accept the subtle opportunity of escape that's coupled with each trial. We all have our weaknesses, and our ever-present Father is always near so you won't have to resist alone—take the help.

1 CORINTHIANS 10:12–13 (NLT)

> If you think you are standing strong, be careful not to fall. The temptations in your life are no different from what others experience. And God is faithful. He will not allow the temptation to be more than you can stand. When you are tempted, He will show you a way out so that you can endure.

THE FATHER HELPS YOU DO WHAT YOU CAN'T DO ALONE

N	H	D	N	C	U	T	N	G	C	A	N	Y	B	E
J	X	Q	E	O	M	E	V	G	Q	Y	H	L	N	B
E	K	D	E	N	V	S	C	B	B	Y	E	I	I	B
J	H	Q	G	O	Y	E	E	X	C	E	L	A	O	P
H	F	A	T	H	E	R	R	S	V	P	P	D	Z	A
F	B	P	M	I	B	J	A	C	I	O	L	E	K	X
T	D	L	M	F	O	U	T	C	O	M	E	S	O	G
E	D	D	O	P	S	B	S	O	U	M	O	I	N	C
U	K	Q	Y	X	I	I	T	N	K	V	E	R	U	L
G	Q	O	R	Z	D	P	R	F	O	D	H	E	P	C
V	F	U	Q	G	D	Q	U	L	M	Y	S	O	H	S
Y	U	X	K	J	F	W	G	I	C	Y	V	K	M	X
V	W	H	I	G	R	Q	G	C	G	B	C	I	L	V
W	S	I	M	I	L	B	L	T	O	M	X	Y	F	U
N	P	R	O	D	U	C	E	S	B	G	Q	L	F	K

- STRUGGLE
- HELP
- EXCEL
- DENY
- LURE
- DISOBEY
- DAILY
- DISCIPLINE
- PRODUCES
- DESIRED
- OUTCOMES
- OVERCOME
- CONFLICTS
- FATHER
- PROMISES

LESSON #48

Everything In The House Belongs To The Father, He Can Do As He Pleases

It's almost comical, but if you know anything about my family by now, you should know my daughters and I eat eggs for breakfast. They are a quick-fix meal that everyone can eat together, everyone loves, and I can make a big batch at once for all to gather around and enjoy. This day, I got up early and fed the girls their morning meal first; then I sat down with a plate of eggs that was custom made just for me. As I sat, I could see the quorum beginning to form with their four pleading eyes staring at me. I knew what this meant—this meant they wanted some of my eggs! My eggs were fresh off the skillet, so they were still sizzling and piping hot, but that's okay for me because I can handle hot food.

It wasn't long before I gave into the pressure of their wheedling little eyes, and I blew on a spoonful of eggs to cool them down for the girls. Now the next scoop was all mine, so I ate them hot—not a problem, this is what I do, because I'm the dad. Then again, after eating their biteful, they started looking at me again, signaling for more. But this time when I began to blow on the eggs to cool them down, the girls didn't see the difference between me eating more eggs and me cooling them off to give to them. This caused them to start whining and complaining because they thought I was eating all the eggs. Now, may I remind you, these were my eggs to begin with!

So if I decide to share some of what I have or not share any at all, that's my prerogative, and it's my legitimate authority to determine. I then thought to myself, *They need to understand the reality that if I choose to give them some of what's mine, then that's just my fatherly favor towards them.* But regardless of my decision, they don't have the right to complain, because it's all mine. I can either keep it for myself or bring it to a state where they can benefit from, digest, and enjoy it with me. If in the process of me blessing them, they have to wait a little while, they shouldn't complain. If they have to wait until I think my blessings are appropriate for their palate, they shouldn't complain. If I choose to not bless them in this area at all, then they must remember that I've already given them enough to sustain them, so as an act of gratefulness, they shouldn't complain. After all, it all belongs to me, and I can do with it whatever I choose.

Those thoughts towards my children reminded me of the sovereignty of Our Father. He is our great provider, the master authority, and our supreme shepherd. As Our Father and the Creator of all things, He's in total control and doesn't owe us the things we desire but rather He sovereignly chooses to bless us daily as an extension of His favor. Even when we don't get what we want, we must learn to appreciate the grace of His restraint. Be encouraged while waiting on Him, even in His delay of "cooling things down" for you; it does not mean He's denying you those very same blessings. I urge you, in your hour of impatience, to not jump the gun and complain. Let's trust Our Father.

1 CHRONICLES 29:11–12 (NLT)

" Yours, O LORD, is the greatness, the power, the glory, the victory, and the majesty. Everything in the heavens and on earth is Yours, O LORD, and this is Your kingdom. We adore You as the one who is over all things. Wealth and honor come from You alone, for You rule over everything. Power and might are in Your hand, and at Your discretion people are made great and given strength.

EVERYTHING IN THE HOUSE BELONGS TO THE FATHER, HE CAN DO AS HE PLEASES

P	T	S	Y	X	Q	R	G	A	K	A	L	G	V	K
K	R	N	T	F	N	P	E	R	C	S	Y	Q	J	Y
K	E	E	I	D	N	S	R	S	W	W	H	D	P	I
P	T	Z	R	A	U	E	D	O	T	D	Z	R	L	K
R	S	W	O	O	R	L	M	V	V	Y	N	E	M	E
B	A	C	H	J	G	T	O	E	Q	I	G	H	N	O
K	M	R	T	A	H	A	S	R	R	I	D	P	Y	S
I	B	E	U	U	M	Z	T	E	T	P	H	E	R	Q
G	K	A	A	T	M	S	Y	I	R	N	U	H	R	Y
O	N	T	Z	X	Z	W	M	G	V	X	O	S	E	A
L	C	O	M	P	L	A	I	N	K	E	Q	C	H	R
X	B	R	L	E	T	H	Z	T	H	D	T	U	T	O
L	J	F	T	E	Y	Y	T	Y	U	C	Y	P	A	R
H	I	Y	O	E	B	D	G	K	I	T	J	N	F	D
D	D	P	W	K	C	U	Q	R	K	U	C	B	I	C

- HOUSE
- BELONG
- PREROGATIVE
- LEGITIMATE
- SOVEREIGNTY
- PROVIDER
- MASTER
- AUTHORITY
- SUPREME
- SHEPHERD
- CREATOR
- CONTROL
- FATHER
- COMPLAIN
- RESTRAINT

LESSON #49

The Fathers Children are In His Hands, On His Mind, and In His Plans

I remember growing up in the small town of Long Beach, CA. The block I lived on was my world. We used to always ride around on our bikes and walk around the neighborhood. I remember always wanting to test the boundaries of how far I could go, but even traveling five or six blocks was super far because in those distant places were dogs, alleys, and stuff I'd never seen before. I remember continually trying to ride my bike farther and farther into the great unknown. I felt like I was going places. Then I went off to college and was like, "Wow not only have I left my block but I've left the city, now I'm really doing big things." From there, I took different jobs, grew in life, and traveled to different countries, so again I found myself thinking, "Wow, there is so much more to this world than I ever knew." If never before, now I was really going places and doing big things.

I was with my daughters, and it was a weekend morning, so the family agenda was a little more relaxed. It's days like these that I would go into their room, close all the doors, take them out of their cribs, and we will just play. With the room enclosed, they are able to roll and do whatever they want within the room with me. I'll just sit there and watch them. If they want to climb up on me, that's okay, and if they want to hug and laugh with me, I'm all in. We play with toys, we clap to a song, we dance to the music of the toys, and we're just in the room doing daddy/daughter time early in the morning.

At one point Jessica, my youngest daughter, got mad at me about something trivial, so she decided to walk away to get away from me. I said to her, "Hey, Jessica, where are you going? This is daddy/daughter time! Our special father/child time. Where are you going?" She turns around to look at me then turns back around and starts as fast as she can heading towards the door. This is what she considers to be running away from me, sprinting towards the way out. So I say, "All right, run from me if you want, but the room door is shut, and you can't open it. So with all the running you're trying to do, you can't get farther than where I'm allowing you to go. Even if you were able to somehow miraculously open the door, the farthest you will be able to run is within the limits of our home. It's there you will find another door with a lock on it that you can't reach or unlock."

It amazes me how she thinks she can run from me, that she can go somewhere out of my presence, out of my reach, or out of my provision for her. It reminds me of these scriptures in Psalm 139:1–10 (NIV):

> You have searched me, LORD, and you know me.
> You know when I sit and when I rise; You perceive my thoughts from afar. You discern my going out and my lying down; You are familiar with all my ways. Before a word is on my tongue You, LORD, know it completely. You hem me in behind and before, and You lay Your hand upon me. Such knowledge is too wonderful for me, too lofty for me to attain. Where can I go from Your Spirit? Where can I flee from your presence? If I go up to the heavens, You are there; if I make my bed in the depths, You are there. If I rise on the wings of the dawn, if I settle on the far side of the sea, even there Your hand will guide me, Your right hand will hold me fast.

I hear Our Father clearly saying, "You are in My hand, you are on My mind, you are in My plans. There is nowhere you can go that I am not there, so stop trying to run from Me. You've been running for too long—running from trust, running from faith, running from responsibility. Stop running. I know where you are because I placed you there and you are in My care. Turn back towards your Father, and run towards Me."

THE FATHERS CHILDREN ARE IN HIS HANDS, ON HIS MIND, AND IN HIS PLANS

C	Y	B	P	O	N	U	I	X	F	V	F	M	S	Q
R	E	V	M	K	X	S	T	D	Z	E	A	U	D	B
K	E	L	X	V	L	X	R	I	D	M	V	Q	L	G
F	D	S	T	O	P	O	T	H	N	T	N	L	Q	I
B	I	J	P	S	L	T	F	A	I	T	H	W	I	V
U	U	Z	P	O	A	R	S	N	M	E	O	S	B	L
D	G	N	I	N	N	U	R	D	Z	K	E	F	B	G
X	C	B	Z	P	S	S	P	S	E	A	E	A	Z	R
G	T	A	K	S	U	T	I	Y	W	P	Y	R	N	V
I	N	F	P	O	I	J	T	B	S	E	T	T	K	V
J	B	D	P	J	I	P	N	C	I	E	I	H	F	F
I	Z	W	Q	D	P	B	X	V	A	L	R	E	S	P
I	W	C	E	I	S	H	S	Q	Z	F	I	S	O	W
B	U	Q	Z	M	E	N	I	W	X	W	P	T	D	J
D	H	N	I	H	A	C	R	D	A	V	S	L	Y	F

- HANDS
- MIND
- PLANS
- RUNNING
- FAITH
- TRUST
- RESPONSIBILITY
- FLEE
- FARTHEST
- SEA
- STOP
- DEPTHS
- GUIDE
- SPIRIT
- LORD

LESSON #50

The Father Loves to Hear the Voices of His Children

My oldest daughter, Johannah, has been diagnosed with a developmental delay, so she isn't coherently vocal yet (thank God for the "yet"). I am extremely grateful for my renewed faith in the anticipation of "yet." There are many typical things she previously couldn't do "yet" but now is able to do, so this "yet" when it comes to speech will also come to pass!

Johannah is three years old, and the extent of her verbal abilities is her making the sound "ack," similar to the quack of a duck but without the "qu." She punches this word very loudly to get the attention she needs and also uses it as a method of general communication. Along with her "ack," she has a hum sound like "hmm" when she likes the way something tastes or wants more food to eat.

When I drop my girls off at daycare around 9:30 a.m., it's the time when the rest of their classes are having recess. So I drop the girls off first, Jessica then Johannah, then I go back to the car and grab their bags because it's too risky to carry everything at once. By the time I place their bags in their class, Johannah will no longer be there because her teachers will have taken her out for recess. During recess, I hear a yard full of young three-year-olds playing, screaming, running, yelling, laughing, and just making all kinds of wonderful expressions. I can hear the yard full of maybe sixty young voices having a ball. What pleases and amazes me about this audible experience is, among the noise, among the laughter, and among the play, I can hear "ack," "ack," "ack"!

I hear her, and it sounds like she's having fun! She's able to contribute her noise to the youthful ruckus that's echoing off the walls. I can pick up in her tone that she's doing what she knows to do to express the same amount of pleasure and exuberance as the other children are; it's just that they have more sounds to express their joy. But I know, since I know my daughter, that she's having a blast. She's in her element, she's living life, and she's joyful. Instantly, my soul is comforted. I may not understand it, and she may not sound like the rest of them, but she's my child, and however she vocalizes her joy is music to my ears.

This is how glad Our Father must be when we are in His presence, living out loud, and experiencing life the way He designed it for us. He desires to hear us tell it all to Him when we are going through the joys and trials of our unfolding story and can still acknowledge that through it all, life is good. We should continually give Our Father praise and boldly surrender to Him our best shout. Let Him hear us sound off about His goodness while we are still in the land of the living. We may not sound as beautiful as the other gifted, talented voices may sound. We may not be as melodic or as finely tuned. But whatever our noise is, whatever our squawk may be, let's let Our Father hear us! He desires to hear our voices, our release, our concerns, our thoughts, our worries, and our enthusiasm; all of these are music to His ears. He loves us and our sound just the way we are, so don't hold back. Whether it's praise and worship, let go. In the time of joy, let's go for it. In the time of pain and heartache, let Him hear you. Our Father knows you, and it is you and your unique sound that bring Him joy.

PSALM 100 (ESV)

> Make a joyful noise to the LORD, all the earth! Serve the LORD with gladness! Come into His presence with singing! Know that the LORD, He is God! It is He who made us, and we are His; we are His people, and the sheep of His pasture. Enter His gates with thanksgiving, and His courts with praise! Give thanks to him; bless His name! For the LORD is good; His steadfast love endures forever, and His faithfulness to all generations.

THE FATHER LOVES TO HEAR THE VOICES OF HIS CHILDREN

P	A	S	U	R	R	E	N	D	E	R	K	D	M	G
J	V	B	C	I	L	E	Y	X	M	J	D	W	B	Y
S	J	X	L	J	R	B	U	E	W	N	S	H	S	Y
A	Y	E	E	D	E	B	I	X	D	U	G	V	O	V
L	R	S	L	A	E	M	V	U	L	V	E	K	B	U
R	H	I	I	R	O	O	O	F	O	R	F	C	H	J
E	H	O	A	V	C	L	I	V	I	N	G	I	I	J
C	U	N	Y	A	A	A	C	S	H	I	N	K	U	I
N	C	G	L	A	D	N	E	S	S	O	H	E	D	M
E	U	I	D	A	S	D	S	H	P	E	L	H	R	U
S	Z	Z	L	T	F	N	O	P	O	Y	C	T	U	P
E	L	J	O	Y	F	U	L	F	L	X	W	Z	G	H
R	P	M	B	X	T	O	E	P	Y	J	H	V	M	H
P	G	B	X	X	Z	S	P	H	W	X	O	K	S	A
F	O	H	M	O	S	N	C	I	V	H	N	Z	K	B

- VOICES
- CHILDREN
- PRESENCE
- LIVING
- LOUD
- DESIRE
- BOLDLY
- SURRENDER
- SHOUT
- SOUND
- EXUBERANCE
- VOCALIZE
- JOYFUL
- NOISE
- GLADNESS

LESSON #51

The Father Uses Things to Draw Us Closer

On any given day, there are times when our entire family is in the home but my daughters are kind of far from me and I either want to play with them or be near them. The trouble is I don't want to give up my comfy seat, so I have to be very creative in how I get their attention, or I risk the chance of them avoiding me altogether, thinking it's a type of game.

It's very easy for me to lose their attention because from a child's perspective, there are so many other fun things to do in the house than go to Dad when he calls. There are toys, couches, magazines, tables, book stands, and an array of other everyday items we as parents take for granted, but to children they are an adventure not to be missed!

In order to compete with the playful "noise" of their world and get their attention so they'll come to me, I sometimes have to place a toy that I know they really like or an object of particular interest to them somewhere between where they are and where I am. Then I'll toss the toy (or whatever it is) so it's just outside of their reach but significantly closer to me so they will have to move in my direction to get whatever it is that they think they want. When I see them crawling to get the first object of interest, I either move it closer to me or leave it there but place another, more interesting toy beyond the first one that's even closer to where I am.

Since I'm their father, I know what fascinates them. And since I own all the items in the house, I will continue to use whatever is necessary to pique their interest and draw them closer to me. In the process of me "calling" them through the material stuff,

I'll sometimes let them keep some of the toys I used to compel them. My end goal in allowing them to attain the toys is not for them to have more toys but to eventually bring them closer to their father. Then when they're in my arms' reach, I grab them, swoop them up, kiss all over their cheeks, hug them tight, and we smile and laugh together. After all, all I wanted to do was to love on them in the first place.

Can you see how Our Father works through all sorts of things to get us to accept His relentless love for us? I know at times we mistakenly place a higher priority on the things we can see, the things we have learned to idolize, and the things we think we need to survive far over Our Father's call for us to seek Him first. But I hope we realize that those things lose meaning when compared to having Him as provider, protector, and guide. I pray we learn to take quiet times away from the noise of our busy lives. When we move from our insatiable desires for more stuff and draw nearer to Our Father, we can hear His call for our lives more clearly and accept His love even more readily. This week, draw closer to Him.

ROMANS 8:28 (NLT)

" And we know that God causes everything to work together for the good of those who love God and are called according to his purpose for them.

THE FATHER USES THINGS TO DRAW US CLOSER

H	R	N	L	H	G	M	L	U	L	Y	C	V	P	W
E	B	E	O	J	S	C	Q	P	F	R	P	C	I	U
G	D	A	L	L	L	M	F	G	U	H	O	N	Y	R
S	G	R	F	E	K	A	R	T	I	M	Y	K	X	P
I	P	E	A	E	N	T	B	G	P	V	M	W	A	F
Q	S	R	M	W	V	T	H	E	U	E	I	O	M	H
R	L	A	I	U	M	E	L	E	V	P	C	D	P	Q
Y	C	A	L	O	R	N	R	E	S	O	L	C	Z	N
Q	F	E	Y	S	R	T	V	Y	S	R	L	I	A	F
X	N	Q	X	A	V	I	G	X	D	S	U	N	I	M
X	A	S	K	Y	T	O	T	Z	O	A	T	B	H	X
I	X	F	E	A	B	N	H	Y	U	I	Y	Q	Z	P
P	D	A	E	G	T	O	J	N	C	I	V	Z	K	M
K	J	R	S	C	Z	H	Z	U	K	U	O	Y	T	W
F	C	R	T	M	S	F	C	Q	B	G	D	G	D	O

- FAMILY
- CREATIVE
- ATTENTION
- EVERYDAY
- DRAW
- CLOSER
- RELENTLESS
- LOVE
- HIGHER
- PRIORITY
- SEEK
- NEARER
- CLEARLY
- ACCEPT
- LOVE
- COMPEL

LESSON #52

Thank You Father

My simplest, most profound prayer and expression of gratitude…thank you.

Volumes could be written to say thank you and still only cover the basic needs You provide, like food, clothes, shelter, and life itself, but You've been better than that. Please accept these few words from my heart.

Thank you for Your presence and Your still, small voice that has always been with me, even as a child. Thank You for the times when I drowned out that voice but You tolerated my cold heart because You felt I was too important to let go.

Thank you for all of the angels You've sent me along the way so far. I have a bad habit of placing myself in terrible situations, but You have given me confidence through the night, courage in a fight, and a listening ear when I have seemingly lost it all. Thank You for Your forgiveness.

Thank you for the many men You have sent my way to help me piece together what a real man should be. Thank you for providing examples of justice, boldness, meekness, commitment, integrity, leadership, strength, and love through both men and women to give guidance to my inner man.

Thank you for my mother. She's a rock, a warrior, a pray-er, and a tireless helper. Because of her, I believe anything is possible. Thank you for taking care of my three siblings and me as we grew up with the everyday traps of poverty and life in the inner city.

Thank you for revealing Yourself to me by Your Spirit and Your Word, through Christ, and for showing me the purpose You created me to accomplish. Your confidence in me reminds me that where I am is not where I am going.

Now that I have a family of my own, thank you for giving me the ability to love my wife and father my children the way You care for me.

Thank you for being my first true love, my superhero, and my peace.

Thank you for always being there.
You made me the man I am today.
Thank you for Your promises that give me hope for tomorrow.
I look forward to seeing You in eternity.
And above all, thank you for teaching me how to love.

1 THESSALONIANS 5:18 (NLT)

> Be thankful in all circumstances, for this is God's will for you who belong to Christ Jesus.

THANK YOU FATHER

P	V	E	W	U	L	Y	W	D	R	P	C	B	Z	E
K	K	K	D	Q	Z	W	Y	H	E	T	W	Y	J	D
F	P	G	O	I	J	H	T	G	Y	X	L	T	L	B
A	Y	M	R	C	V	G	I	Q	A	W	Z	T	S	B
L	N	G	E	A	N	O	N	Z	R	I	D	X	F	C
A	O	Q	H	E	T	I	R	I	P	S	Y	L	O	H
X	S	M	R	W	K	I	E	P	S	H	H	N	R	R
Y	L	T	E	C	A	N	T	L	Y	O	F	P	G	C
A	S	V	P	Q	R	H	E	U	O	I	P	O	I	Q
U	C	O	U	R	A	G	E	S	D	R	A	A	V	N
H	Y	F	S	N	N	P	R	E	S	E	N	C	E	E
U	M	V	K	A	Y	Y	N	O	E	N	N	J	N	R
Q	S	S	J	X	F	C	K	M	K	O	C	H	E	I
Y	Q	W	Q	J	E	S	U	S	C	H	R	I	S	T
J	P	M	J	N	N	A	F	A	Z	Z	L	B	S	A

- PRAYER
- GRATITUDE
- THANKS
- PROVIDE
- PRESENCE
- ANGELS
- CONFIDENCE
- COURAGE
- FORGIVENESS
- MEEKNESS
- STRENGTH
- JESUS CHRIST
- HOLY SPIRIT
- SUPERHERO
- ETERNITY

Conclusion

I PRAY THIS book has been profitable and that you have begun to reap the rewards from the lessons God gives us through the lives of children. I really hope you have tasted the unique freedom that comes from turning the hearts of fathers back to their children and nudging our hearts, as children, back to Our Heavenly Father.

The *Fathers and Children* book is only the beginning of the journey towards what is needed to achieve the positive, peaceful paternal relationships that we were designed to thrive in. I invite you to join me in this critical conversation by adding to the collective roadmap by joining our Facebook group and posting your own inspired thoughts and stories about fatherhood.

Stay in touch with people that are believing and living out the call God has placed on our lives as fathers and children. Visit us at www.FATHERSandChildrenBOOK.com anytime for information on where to find us, conversations about fatherhood, and other supportive services.

This IS the day the LORD has made, make it a GREAT one!

CERTIFICATE
OF ACHIEVEMENT

THIS CERTIFICATE IS PROUDLY PRESENTED TO

....

You have successfully completed the Fathers and Childrens Book and are now officially a part of the family.

Be sure to join our Facebook Group. There you can share and discuss your takeaways from the Fathers and Children book as well as post a picture and share your own fatherhood moments. Keep checking the website to get a printable copy of this certificate with your name on it, it should be available soon. I pray Godspeed, tremendous success, and true happiness in your pursuit to fulfill God's calling on your life!

Kyron Jackson

Kyron Jackson, Author, Fathers and Children

10 WAYS TO BE A GOOD DAD*

1. RESPECT YOUR CHILDREN'S MOTHER
One of the best things a father can do for his children is to respect their mother.

2. SPEND TIME WITH YOUR CHILDREN
How a father spends his time tells his children what's important to him.

3. LISTEN FIRST, TALK SECOND
All too often the only time a father speaks to his children is when they have done something wrong. Take time and listen to their ideas and problems.

4. DISCIPLINE WITH LOVE
All children need guidance and discipline, not as punishment, but to set reasonable limits.

5. BE A ROLE MODEL
Fathers are role models to their kids whether they realize it or not.

6. BE A TEACHER
A father who teaches his children about right and wrong, and encourages them to do their best, will see his children make good choices.

7. EAT TOGETHER AS A FAMILY
Sharing a meal together (breakfast, lunch or dinner) can be an important part of healthy family life.

8. READ TO YOUR CHILDREN
It is important that fathers make the effort to read to their children.

9. SHOW AFFECTION
Children need the security that comes from knowing they are wanted, accepted and loved by their fathers.

10. REALIZE THAT A FATHER'S JOB IS NEVER DONE
Even after children are grown and ready to leave home, they will still look to their fathers for wisdom and advice.

*National Fatherhood Institute

Pictures

Jackson Family Downtown Los Angeles

Jackson Family Having Fun at the Park

Kyron and Johannah

Kyron and Jessica

Kyron and Daughters Johannah and Jessica at LA County Fair

United States President Barack Obama and his daughters, Malia, left, and Sasha. Photography by Pete Souza.

Bruce Lee with son Brandon

Former National Baseball League player Jackie Robinson with his son at a Civil Rights March on Washington, D.C

Ernest Hemingway with sons Patrick (left) and Gregory (right) with kittens in Finca Vigia, Cuba

President John F. Kennedy with children. Hyannisport Weekend. Photography by Cecil (Cecil William) Stoughton.

*Sean (P.Diddy) Combs and his children Christian and Justin.
Photograhy by David Shankbone*

Index

A
Ability   32, 60, 76, 79, 112, 184
Accept   208
Acceptance   44, 76, 95
Accepted   132
Accountable   48
Adam   40
Advance   64
Affirm   168
Again   172
Always   175
Angels   212
Anger   55
Anointing   184
Appreciate   164
Arranges   8
Ask   140
Attention   68, 100, 208
Attentive   124
Attitude   128, 164
Audience   184
Authority   196
Aware   40

B
Battle   156
Behavior   40, 128
Belief   76
Believers   92
Belong   112, 196
Benefit   24, 55, 112
Better   76
Beyond   64
Blame   84
Blessing   79, 108, 132, 164
Blocks   100
Boldly   204
Boldness   79
Boundaries   24

Bring   140
Brute   112

C
Call   68
Can   36
Capable   172
Capacity   32
Care   8, 11, 144, 175
Catastrophe   72
Celebration   168
Changing   115
Character   48, 128
Cherubim   24
Childlike   164
Children   100, 140, 148, 204
Choice   95
Circumstances   68
Clearly   208
Close   55, 72
Closeness   152
Closer   44, 208
Comfort   16, 36, 187
Command   24, 95
Commandments   128
Communicate   48
Comparisons   164
Compassion   44, 60
Compel   68, 208
Complain   196
Complaining   164
Composure   128
Compromise   128
Concerns   160
Condition   28, 52
Conduct   128
Confess   88
Confidence   79, 168, 212

Confirmation   168
Conflicts   191
Confuse   64
Connection   20, 168
Conquer   156
Consistency   76
Constant   8, 11, 115
Contribution   108
Control   196
Conversation   36
Correct   44
Correction   88, 95
Courage   212
Covenant   120
Coworkers   92
Creative   208
Creator   88, 196
Cry   100, 156, 175
Curiosity   68
Curious   36

D
Daily   140, 180, 191
Damaging   120
Dangers   79
Decide   40
Delight   184
Delivers   175
Deny   191
Dependable   115
Dependence   8, 152
Depths   200
Designed   8, 112
Desire   20, 76, 120, 180, 204
Desired   191
Desperate   175
Details   160
Detours   120
Development   79
Devoted   132
Direction   115
Discern   76
Discipleship   124

Discipline   55, 191
Discover   68
Disobey   191
Distance   55
Divine   112
Door   72, 120
Drama   160
Draw   208
Drive   168
Duty   24
Dwell   152

E
Eden   40
Embody   20
Embrace   20, 44
Endure   64
Enemy   156
Engage   92
Enjoy   28
Enjoying   52
Enough   8, 148
Environment   168
Envy   160
Equip   48
Equipped   112
Escape   88
Eternity   212
Every   48
Everyday   136, 208
Everyone   148
Everything   136
Everywhere   88
Evidence   124
Evil   24
Example   48, 92
Exceeds   76
Excel   191
Exercise   20
Experience   60, 168, 172
Explore   168
Exuberance   204

F

Face 132
Faith 132, 200
Faithful 148
Familiarity 16
Family 11, 208
Farthest 200
Father 8, 60, 68, 72, 84, 100, 104, 115, 120, 124, 140, 144, 152, 164, 168, 175, 191, 196
Fatherhood 48, 55, 108
Favor 104, 108, 148
Fear 52
Fed 124
Feed 124
Feet 152
Fight 156
Filled 8
Finger 24
Flee 200
Focus 144
Follow 36, 104
Forever 187
Forgiveness 44, 88, 212
Formula 16
Friends 92
Frustration 55
Fulfill 140
Future 20, 92

G

Gain 68
Gather 148
Generations 11
Generosity 132
Gift 79, 136, 184
Give 84
Gladness 204
Glorify 104
Glory 184
Good 24, 48
Goodness 187
Grabs 152
Grace 44, 136, 168
Gracious 132
Grandeur 20
Grateful 60, 180
Gratitude 164, 212
Great 95
Greatness 115
Grin 132
Grounded 115
Grow 32, 104, 108, 180
Guards 160
Guidance 104, 108
Guide 44, 52, 187, 200

H

Habits 32
Hand 11, 52, 115, 152, 200
Handle 136
Hard 8
Harmful 120
Heal 175
Healthy 16
Hearing 100
Heart 40, 152, 160, 180
Heaven 95
Heavenly 84, 168
Hell 95
Help 191
Hide 84
Higher 64, 208
His 95
Hold 144
Holy 180
Holy Spirit 212
Home 8
Honor 187
Hope 92
House 196
Humble 152
Hurts 32

I

Identity 20
Improves 55
Influence 92
Insecurities 88
Inspire 115
Instruct 44
Instruction 24, 48, 68
Integrity 128
Intended 16, 112
Intent 40
Intervene 88
Intervention 120
Intimate 60
Inventory 40
Investigate 68
Involvement 11

J

Jesus Christ 212
Journey 79, 144
Joy 108, 132, 140
Joyful 204
Judgment 76

K

Kingdom 84, 124
Know 48, 175

L

Learn 55, 72, 180
Learning 44
Leg 120
Legitimate 196
Level 60
Liberates 175
Liberty 24, 44
Life 28, 79, 115
Light 124
Likeness 20
Limitations 32
Limits 52
Listening 55, 100

Listens 175
Living 92, 204
Lord 64, 200
Loud 204
Love 36, 40, 88, 128, 144, 152, 187, 208
Loving 100, 132
Lure 191

M

Magnify 184
Master 196
Mature 2
Maturity 3
Maximize 108
Measured 148
Meekness 212
Memory 172
Mending 11
Mercy 44, 136
Mess 128
Might 124
Mind 200
Mindset 140
Minimize 108
Ministry 92
Mirror 20
Mistakes 44
Model 104
Move 180
Muscle 112

N

Near 175
Nearby 40
Nearer 208
Needed 148
Needs 32, 52, 60
Never 100
Noise 100, 204
Nothing 36
Noticed 132

O

Obedience   24
Obey   72, 95, 128
Observing   100
Ointment   11
Okay   28
Omer   148
Omnipresent   52
Oneness   180
Open   72
Operate   184
Opportunity   24, 40, 72
Optimistic   20
Others   124, 164
Outcomes   191
Overcome   79, 191
Overflow   187
Overpowering   112
Overwhelm   148

P

Path   28
Pathway   60
Patience   28, 104
Patient   16
Pattern   36
Peace   132, 136, 160, 180, 187
People   84, 100
Permission   168
Personal   32, 52
Pitfalls   108
Places   92
Plan   28, 164, 200
Pleased   168
Pleasing   132
Pleasure   184
Plenty   148
Portion   136, 148
Position   112, 156
Positive   140
Potential   20
Power   112
Practice   104, 164

Praise   184
Pray   72
Prayer   115, 140, 172, 180, 212
Preparation   144
Prepare   48, 187
Prepared   112
Prerogative   196
Presence   36, 88, 204, 212
Presentation   144
Prevent   164
Pride   88
Priority   208
Problems   88
Process   32, 115
Produces   191
Profitable   48
Promises   191
Prosper   112
Protect   104, 148
Protection   32, 120, 144, 160, 168
Protects   120
Proven   172
Provide   60, 104, 148, 175, 212
Providence   112
Provider   152, 196
Provision   32, 144, 172
Purpose   16

Q

Questions   64

R

Reach   68
Ready   76
Realize   104, 164
Recognition   76
Recognize   8
Redeemer   180
Refilling   11
Reflection   20
Regardless   32
Reinforce   128

Rejoice   95
Relate   60
Relationship   24, 40, 52, 92, 120, 136, 172
Relentless   208
Reliable   172
Reliance   8, 76
Rely   108
Remain   55, 140
Remember   8, 16, 40, 48
Remind   8, 28
Remove   84
Renew   187
Repentance   16
Residue   11
Resources   100
Responds   175
Responsibility   79, 136, 200
Responsible   16, 24
Rest   152, 187
Restocks   136
Restore   88, 175
Restraint   196
Return   95
Returned   95
Revelation   64
Roar   168
Rock   8
Rotten   16
Running   68, 84, 200

S

Safe   115, 180
Safeguard   120
Scope   64
Sea   200
Seamless   11
Seasons   16
Secure   115
Seeing   164
Seek   68, 208
Seizure   28
Selfish   124

Separate   36
Serenity   180
Serve   124
Shaking   28
Sharing   92
Sheep   36
Shepherd   36, 187, 196
Shine   132
Short   172
Shout   204
Shrink   79
Shut   72
Sing   152
Situation   84, 140
Skills   184
Slow   55
Small   72
Smile   28, 184
Smiling   100, 132
Solution   108
Son   60, 68
Sound   204
Sovereign   64, 160
Sovereignty   112, 196
Speak   140
Speaking   55
Spirit   72, 88, 200
Stand   156
Still   72
Stimulate   28
Stop   84, 144, 200
Strength   52, 79, 187, 212
Stress   160
Stretch   108
Strong   156
Struggle   88, 191
Submit   84
Success   32, 52
Suited   76
Superhero   212
Support   52
Supreme   196
Surrender   152, 204

Swagger 44
Sword 120
Symbol 128

T
Talents 184
Tambourine 184
Tears 156
Temperament 128
Temporary 120
Temptations 60
Tender 44
Term 172
Tested 60
Testimony 172
Thanks 212
Things 84
Thoughts 64
Timely 144
Timing 16, 64
Together 180
Touch 11
Training 52
Transfer 11
Trials 136
Trouble 55, 172
Trust 11, 16, 28, 36, 40, 76, 84, 92, 104, 128, 144, 160, 172, 200
Trusting 52
Turbulence 28

U
Unashamed 184
Understand 24, 48, 60
Understanding 32, 64, 68, 72
Unique 55, 175
United 180
Unity 20
Unknown 148
Urgent 172

V
Valley 187
Vestibular 28
Victory 156
Vocalize 204
Voice 36, 72, 95, 156, 204

W
Wait 144
Walk 124
Wants 32
War 156
Warm 115
Warrior 156
Water 120
Whatever 140
Whimper 156
Whining 164
Whole 11
Wisdom 16, 76, 144, 160
Wisely 92
Wiser 79, 108
Withstand 136
Word 36, 140
Work 48, 136
World 100
Worship 152
Worth 20

Y
Yes 64
Yourself 124

Z
Zeal 64

For more from Kyron Jackson, go to
www.FATHERSandChildrenBOOK.com

- **Like Facebook Fan Page:** FATHERSandChildrenBOOK
- **Join Facebook Group:** FATHERSandChildrenBOOK
- **Follow on Twitter:** @FatherChildBOOK #FatherChildBook

www.ingramcontent.com/pod-product-compliance
Lightning Source LLC
LaVergne TN
LVHW041540070426
835507LV00011B/846